# ROUGH DIAMONDS

Paul Bradbridge

Brydget Foreman.

# Rough Diamonds

Twenty-one Uncut Sketches from
Riding Lights Roughshod Theatre Company

## EDITED BY PAUL BURBRIDGE

MONARCH
BOOKS

Mill Hill, London NW7 3SA and Grand Rapids, Michigan

First published by Monarch Books in the UK 2001,
Concorde House, Grenville Place,
Mill Hill, London, NW7 3SA.

Published in the USA by Monarch Books 2001.

Distributed by:
UK: STL, PO Box 300, Kingstown Broadway, Carlisle,
Cumbria CA3 0QS;
USA: Kregel Publications, PO Box 2607
Grand Rapids, Michigan 49501.

ISBN 1 85424 518 X (UK)
ISBN 0 8254 6017 4 (USA)

**British Library Cataloguing Data**
A catalogue record for this book is available
from the British Library.

Book design and production for the publishers by
Bookprint Creative Services
P.O. Box 827, BN21 3YJ, England
Printed in Great Britain.

# LICENCE TO PERFORM
# THE SKETCHES IN THIS BOOK

4. The licence does *not* confer the right to reproduce the text, or part of the text, in any form. *(See the publisher's copyright note at the front of the book.)*

5. Acknowledgements of any performance in programmes (where applicable) should mention the title of the book, the authors and publishers.

6. All recording rights are reserved and are subject to separate negotiation.

7. Licence applications should be posted to *Rough Diamonds*, P.O. Box 223, YORK, YO1 1GW, sent with a cheque, stating the name and address to which the licence should be issued.

All cheques should be made out in pounds sterling and made payable to *'Rough Diamonds'*.

*NB*
*The above refers to Amateur Performances (to both paying and non-paying audiences). A separate application should be made to the same address by any professional company wishing to perform this material. Permission to perform will involve either a fee or the payment of a royalty on box-office receipts.*

*Please note that applications for Performing Licences relating to other books by the same authors should be accompanied by separate cheques (made out to the title of the relevant book) and sent to the address specified in that book.*

For
Chris and Christine

. . . the common people heard him gladly.

Mark's Gospel

# CONTENTS

# INTRODUCTION

This latest collection of sketches from Riding Lights, *Rough Diamonds*, has a number of important facets. Perhaps the most reassuring one to somebody coming fresh to this book is that each script has been thoroughly tested in performance. These performances have been given by the Riding Lights' *Roughshod* Theatre Companies – professional community touring companies of young actors working in all kinds of venues, including theatres, churches, schools, prisons and other more unusual places such as naval bases, cafés and offices. So these scripts come with at least one guarantee: they have already been used to communicate with all kinds of people across the country. Adults and young people have been moved to laughter, to tears or to indifference – but some will have understood the spiritual heart of the message and responded gladly.

Each year, Riding Lights forms new *Roughshod* companies which generate more new sketch material than we could (or would want to) publish. The twenty-one pieces reproduced here have proved to be dependable 'diamonds' to which we return again and again. Some flaws will certainly remain but other groups of performers may find ways to overcome them in their rehearsals. The diamonds will continue to be cut and polished.

Another encouraging facet of this book from my point of view is the number of writers who have contributed to this collection. I counted eleven. Ever since the grassroots work of Riding Lights Theatre Company was revived by the advent of our *Roughshod* community companies in 1992, our creativity has benefited enormously from an influx of young talent and fresh energy. Our patterns of work have developed and we have been able to foster a lively ensemble atmosphere in the rehearsal room which has resulted in this collective feel to *Rough Diamonds*. In fact, there may be eleven writers who are officially represented, but all of the fifty or so actors who have been part of our *Roughshod* companies for the past eight years have played a part in shaping the material, coming up with original ideas and defining the characters. The creative channels have become more organic. For instance, a number of these sketches started life in improvisation workshops, where characters and ideas were developed by the actors to a point at which a more experienced writer could come in and turn them into a rehearsal script. *Rough Diamonds* is therefore a Company book and contains a broad vein of story-telling material which is ideally suited to ensemble performance.

The name *Roughshod* was not chosen to imply insensitivity, but rather to connect our work with the original meaning of a blacksmith, who would sometimes nail a horse's hooves 'roughly' to give it extra grip in slippery conditions. As a theatre company, we have certainly not always been so surefooted in difficult conditions, but despite this, we have persevered in our aim that *Roughshod* should give performances in communities where life is not very smooth and where theatre itself is rare. We like the 'roughness' which this has given to our theatre – plonking it down in virtually any space, for all kinds of audiences – and we have ourselves been strengthened by the enthusiasm and the honesty of the response we have received. In a sense, those audiences in community halls, schools and prisons have also influenced the nature of the material in this book.

It was said of Jesus that 'the common people heard him gladly' (Mark 12:37). Ordinary people loved to listen to him and were entertained by him. Jesus obviously enjoyed talking to them as well. Maybe his style of communication – popular, entertaining, with a spiritual heart and making people glad – should set the standard for us. I hope that you will find all those ingredients in the following pages, not least the kind of comedy which does people good.

There has always been one particular story in the Gospels which has for me brought together Jesus' passionate love of ordinary people and his sense of humour. It is the story which Luke records in his Gospel about the delightful encounter on the road to Emmaus – the subject of one of the scripts in this book. Of all the material in the Gospels which might suggest comic potential, this famous incident of Jesus appearing to two otherwise unremarkable disciples on their way home after the crucifixion (Luke 24) seems to contain the largest measure of comedy in its original narrative. The Gospel writer relishes the fun to be had from the resurrected Jesus suddenly popping up and holding an extended conversation with people overcome by the sadness of his death at Calvary. The two disciples are in the depths of despair because Jesus is dead and yet *we know* that Jesus is actually walking along beside them. It is a situation full of dramatic irony and ripe for comedy. Luke sets it up: 'they were talking with each other about everything that had happened . . . when Jesus himself came up and walked along with them'.

It becomes genuinely funny when Jesus appears to play along with the joke: 'He asked them, "What are you discussing together as you walk along?" . . . They stood still, their faces downcast and one of them said to Jesus, "You must be the only person in

Jerusalem who does not know the things that have been going on there in the last few days.'" The disciple is astonished at 'Jesus'' ignorance; he almost reprimands 'Jesus' for not keeping abreast of the news . . . about Jesus. And Jesus, who of course is the only person who really *does* know what has been happening over the past few days, not just in Jerusalem but in heaven and in hell as well, plays the situation along a bit further. He refuses to reveal himself and asks nonchalantly (as if butter wouldn't melt in his mouth), 'What things?'

And so a lengthy conversation develops. The failure of the two disciples to recognise Jesus is rather remarkable. It continues for quite a while as the little party trudges all the way back to their front door in Emmaus. It is a full-blown resurrection appearance, this one. Luke tells us that there is even time over the course of the afternoon for a complete study guide, 'beginning with Moses and all the prophets', of everything the Scriptures say about Jesus . . . a Bible study given, of course, by Jesus.

The whole episode is beautifully and amusingly constructed. It develops unerringly towards its punchline, when Jesus breaks bread at their own supper table and (at last!) they recognise him, whereupon he suddenly vanishes from the table. This you would think is a perfectly warm, satisfying and delightful conclusion to the story. However, there is a further twist in the tale, which provides an additional punchline. The two disciples, once the shekel has finally dropped, rush back to Jerusalem, spurred along by an incredible surge of excitement, not only at the reality of the resurrection but that Jesus should have spent the whole afternoon 'talking to them!' 'in what must surely be a very busy resurrection schedule!' 'He even sat down at our supper table for five minutes! . . . but then, sadly, he had to leave.' They obviously thought that Jesus could not have had time to appear to his main inner circle of disciples, so they decided to save him the bother by spreading the news themselves.

So they rush back up the road to Jerusalem in the middle of the night to be the first to spill the beans to this key group of leading disciples. They find them gathered together in one room. Maybe they have to announce themselves by whispering through a locked door: 'Sorry to disturb you. It's Cleopas and Anna. From Emmaus. We know it's late but we've actually got a bit of some rather tremendously exciting news which you might like to hear . . . if you don't mind letting us in.' And, of course, even as they are in the process of describing their encounter with Jesus – well, we have now come to expect the comic timing to be perfect – 'Jesus himself stood among them and said, "Peace be with you."' The first century equivalent of 'Hi!'. It's brilliantly done. And it also gives a bit of encouraging support to those of us who love to bring out the laughter in our faith. I sincerely hope that whoever chooses to rehearse and perform some of these 'rough diamonds' will have lots of fun.

*Paul Burbridge*
Friargate Theatre, YORK
December 2000

# Diamond Geezer
## by Paul Birch and Sally Austen

KEVIN *a bouncer*
WITNEY *a bouncer*
TWO CELEBRITIES ENTERING A CLUB (*walk-on . . . and walk-off again roles*)

One of the most remarkable things about the stories told by Jesus is their resilience. They appear to withstand any amount of retelling and reworking in vastly different cultures and centuries. In their original form, they were memorable ways of communicating a spiritual truth. The stories had power because they described the lives of the audience. People identified with the characters and therefore stood more chance of understanding the spiritual truths which Jesus wanted them to grasp. These truths are timeless; the details of the stories are not, so it is important for us to spend creative energy searching for the new stories and the modern characters in which to dress those same key spiritual ideas for *our* contemporaries.

Here is one such attempt. Hiding inside this duologue is the well-known story of the good Samaritan – the person who set aside prejudice and personal safety in order to show love to a fellow human being. As you will quickly realise, *Diamond Geezer* bears very little resemblance to Jesus' story about robbers and donkeys. Its only obvious connection is the narrative structure of three people who come across an injured man: the two you expect to show compassion walk on, but unexpectedly the third and least likely person stops to help. The context of this sketch is a robust, violent, media-conscious modern world of night-clubs and tabloid journalists. It was written shortly after the death of Princess Diana in a car crash in a Parisian underpass, pursued at high speed by newspaper paparazzi. Hence the identification of the Samaritan with an 'unscrupulous' press hound.

In countless performances in prisons and (even more intimi-dating) secondary school assemblies, the earthy bluntness of this sketch has proved its worth. Sacrificial love has gained a hearing even in situations where tenderness is traditionally despised.

# Diamond Geezer

TWO BOUNCERS, *Kevin and Witney, stand outside a club, their eyes roving to and fro. Two celebrities, shielding themselves from fans and photographers, cross the stage and 'enter' the club.*

| | |
|---|---|
| WITNEY | Evening, Posh. |
| KEVIN | All right, then, Becks? (*Turning on the photographers*) 'Ere! Give us that! (*Grabs imaginary camera and destroys it*) Off yer go! |
| WITNEY | (*Similarly intimidating*) Scum!<br>(*Things calm down again. They return to their posts, eyes flicking around nervously*)<br>D'you have a good night, then, last night? |
| WITNEY | Eventful, as it happens. |
| KEVIN | Oh yeah? Why's that, then? |
| WITNEY | Well, look at the state of my face, Kev. You think I got this shopping at Safeway? |
| KEVIN | (*In shock*) What happened to you? You get done over? |
| WITNEY | Well, as it happens, Kev, it's quite a fascinating little story. |
| KEVIN | Oh yeah? Tell on, Witney. Tell on. |
| WITNEY | Well, I was coming out of The Dog and Duck after a night with good old Jack. (*Mimes knocking back a few drinks*) |
| KEVIN | Jack? |
| WITNEY | Yeh, Jack. Jack Daniels. |
| KEVIN | (*Catching on*) Oh yeah. (*Impersonates Paul Daniels*) 'And that's magic!' |
| WITNEY | (*Ignoring this stupidity*) And there was a great big |

|  | tank of a fella waiting outside . . . |
| KEVIN | Oh yeah . . . |
| WITNEY | And before I knew what had hit me . . . he hit me! |
| KEVIN | Oh no! So what'd you do then? |
| WITNEY | Well, he grabbed me like this, by the hooter . . . |

(*Witney grabs Kevin by the nose*)

KEVIN     Yeah . . .

WITNEY     And he brings me round in front of him like this . . .

(*She brings Kevin round in front of herself so that Kevin's back is to the audience*)

KEVIN     Yeah . . .

WITNEY     And would you believe it – he did this!

KEVIN     What?

WITNEY     This!

(*Kicks Kevin in the groin. Kevin sinks to the ground with an awful groan*)

WITNEY     Bloomin' hurt, it did an' all.

KEVIN     (*In pain*) I can imagine . . . yeah.

WITNEY     No – it *really* hurt!

KEVIN     (*Getting up*) I know!

WITNEY     Nasty.

KEVIN     (*Through gritted teeth*) I know!

WITNEY     So there I was, writhing in agony, when – would you believe it – this other geezer, even bigger than the last one . . .

KEVIN     Oh yeah . . .

WITNEY     Oh yeah. He comes up to me and he grabs me by the scruff of the neck.

KEVIN     (*Fascinated*) Oh yeah . . .

WITNEY     Just like this . . .

(*Grabs Kevin by the neck*)

WITNEY     Then brings me round in front of him like this.

|   |   |
|---|---|
| | (*She brings Kevin round in front again*) |
| KEVIN | (*Following all this*) Right. |
| WITNEY | Right. And before I could say Ginger Spice – Blam! |
| KEVIN | Blam? |
| WITNEY | Blam!! |
| | (*Witney headbutts Kevin, who falls to the ground*) |
| WITNEY | I felt quite ill. |
| KEVIN | (*From the floor*) I can imagine you did. |
| WITNEY | I was in a right state! |
| KEVIN | Nnngghh. |
| WITNEY | But that wasn't all, Kev. |
| KEVIN | (*Alarmed*) Uh?! |
| WITNEY | Just when I thought the coast was clear, this great big gladiator of a bloke . . . |
| KEVIN | (*Nervous and high-pitched*) Yeah? |
| WITNEY | Picks me up by the lug-hole . . . |
| | (*Witney picks up Kevin by the ear*) |
| KEVIN | Yeah? |
| WITNEY | Spins me round . . . |
| | (*She spins Kevin round*) |
| KEVIN | (*High whine*) Yeah? |
| WITNEY | Then . . . he takes my wallet! |
| KEVIN | (*Collapsing with relief*) You were lucky, then! |
| WITNEY | You ain't heard the half of it. |
| KEVIN | (*Moving away quickly*) No? |
| WITNEY | No. So – I'm lying half dead in the gutter when good old PC Dawson comes along. |
| KEVIN | He's a nice bloke, him. |
| WITNEY | Pillar of the community. He comes along . . . |
| KEVIN | And? |
| WITNEY | Walks straight past me like I'm Scotch mist. |
| KEVIN | He doesn't? |

| | |
|---|---|
| WITNEY | He does! |
| KEVIN | He doesn't!? |
| WITNEY | He bloomin' well does! So I'm stuck there, ain't I? Bleeding all over the shop, thinking, I'm done for. Then I just couldn't believe my eyes! |
| KEVIN | Why's that, then? |
| WITNEY | Well, I see that fat bloke off the telly! |
| KEVIN | What, not the one who walks like this? (*Kevin does an impersonation*) |
| WITNEY | Naah! You're thinking of him off Channel 4. It was that charity bloke. Does all them good causes. Little kids and that. |
| KEVIN | (*Suddenly dawns*) Oh yeah, I got yer! My mum likes him. That was lucky. So what did he do? |
| WITNEY | Well, he comes up to me . . . |
| KEVIN | (*Backing away in case he should be on the receiving end of another violent illustration*) And he takes out his hankie and mops up your blood? |
| WITNEY | No, he – |
| KEVIN | What? He rips his jacket off, tears it into strips and bandages you up like that George Clueless off *ER*? |
| WHITNEY | No! He comes up and – |
| KEVIN | (*Babbling excitedly from nervous tension*) Pulls out a makeshift spanner what he happens to carry, uses his aftershave as a temporary anaesthetic, flips you on your back, slices you open with his pen knife and, in a dramatic and selfless gesture, operates on your wounds with the skill and precision of a Swiss transplant surgeon wot's been trained at that Royal Academy of Slicing an' that – little knowing whether you would live or die and at the same time ringing up the air |

ambulance people to perform a dramatic air-sea rescue!

WITNEY    (*Bemused by all this frantic activity*) Well, no. He just gave me his autograph. I got it here, actually. (*Shows it to Kevin by pulling off an autographed sticking plaster from his cheek. Kevin takes it and tries to decipher it*)

KEVIN    Urgh . . . To Witney . . . loving you . . . lots . . . get well soon . . . love . . . Geoff. (*Sentimentally*) Ah, that's lovely, that, innit?

WITNEY    Then *they* came.

KEVIN    They who?

WITNEY    Them.

KEVIN    Them who?

WITNEY    Them wotsits with the cameras.

KEVIN    Wot, birdwatchers?

WITNEY    Nah, you stupid plonka! Them from the papers . . .

KEVIN    Oh no, not them . . . watcha call 'em?

WITNEY    You know! What's that word? The papers . . . papers . . .

KEVIN    Yeah, they're like an army from the papers . . . Chasin' after yer.

WITNEY    Yeah, that's it! The Pepperami!

KEVIN    Oh yeah. I hate them. Vultures!

WITNEY    Chasing after that Geoff bloke off the telly.

KEVIN    Yeah, the Pepperami. Scavengers! I bet they didn't even stop.

WITNEY    Well, that's just it, Kev. You wouldn't Adam and Eve it – this one bloke . . .

KEVIN    Yeah?

WITNEY    He stops. Comes over . . .

KEVIN    Yeah?

| | |
|---|---|
| WITNEY | With his camera . . . |
| KEVIN | (*Cynical*) Oh yeah . . . You, lyin' there all over the front page. |
| WITNEY | And asks if I'm all right. |
| KEVIN | Typical. |
| WITNEY | No, Kev. (*With deliberate emphasis*) He asks if I'm all right. |
| KEVIN | He asks if you're all right? |
| WITNEY | Yeah! He puts his camera down, takes off his jacket and puts it round me – keep me warm, like. |
| KEVIN | You're kiddin' me! |
| WITNEY | Not only that, but he gets out his flash mobile and calls for an ambulance . . . |
| KEVIN | Yeah? |
| WITNEY | Then he takes out his wallet and gives me every-thing in it – to see that I'm all right. |
| KEVIN | He doesn't!? |
| WITNEY | He does. So there I am. One minute stuffed like a turkey, and the next minute I'm on my way to 'ospital courtesy of Mr Properpasty. |
| KEVIN | That's amazing! |
| WITNEY | It was like he was my bruvva or something. |
| KEVIN | Cor. What a night that was! |
| WITNEY | You're telling me, Kevin! |
| | (*Pause. They resume bouncer-watch with greater concentration*) |
| WITNEY | So, what did you do last night, then? |
| KEVIN | Don't ask. |
| WITNEY | What 'appened? |
| KEVIN | Nightmare! |
| WITNEY | So? |
| KEVIN | Only went and had the poodle clipped, didn't I? See that scratch? |

WITNEY        No.

KEVIN         That's deep, that is . . . Probably infected by now
              . . .

              (*The conversation fades out as they walk off*)

# A Fishy Tale about an Ordinary Bloke
### by Antony Dunn

A GROUP OF ACTORS *one of whom should be identified throughout as . . .*
JONAH *a prophet who thinks he's in need of a holiday*

This and several other sketches in this book are typical of one strand of the Roughshod style. This broadly involves high-energy group story-telling, where a rhythmic narrative text is shared between the actors and set to a percussive beat, produced either vocally or with instruments (both familiar ones and 'found' ones). As the narratives unfold, the various mini-scenes are dramatised with simple actions, mime or choreographed movement to illustrate the words. Generally, we have left this 'staging' to your creative imagination, though a few key moments of action have been indicated in the stage directions. Actor-produced sound effects are another useful ingredient, as here at the beginning of the sketch, to conjure up the seaside atmosphere of Jonah's home town.

# A Fishy Tale about an Ordinary Bloke

Once upon a time, on an ordinary day,
an ordinary bloke, in his workaday way,
was walking round Joppa, a seaside town
of very little interest and no renown.
Jonah was the name of this typical guy
who was very much surprised when, up in the
    sky,
the voice of the Lord boomed out of a cloud,
extraordin'rily clearly and extraordin'rily loud,

GOD         Jonah, I've got a job for you,
something extraordin'ry for you to do;
there's a town across the sea, I've seen the sin of
    'er,
so please take a message to the town of
    Nineveh –
'Forty more dinners for the city of sinners,
forty days to change, or it's curtains for Ninners.'

JONAH      But surely this is some kind of elaborate joke –
I'm not a priest or a preacher, just an ordinary
    bloke.

GOD         You'll do.

JONAH      Says who?

GOD         Says me.

JONAH      And you are . . . ?

GOD         I'm God – so get yourself to Ninevaah!

JONAH      OK. Anything you say.

GOD         *GO!*

Jonah heard what God wanted, Jonah agreed,
But Jonah was a yellow-bellied, cowardly weed.

He found himself a boat and he got himself
    afloat,
but he was feeling kinda nervous with a lump in
    his throat,
hoping to escape the Lord's detection
'cos the boat was bound for Tarshish, in the
    opposite direction . . .
from Nineveh.
Hey! Nineveh's *that* way. GO!

JONAH    Ooh, no . . .

ALL    The sea was like a pond – only bigger, of
    course –
but two days later it was bucking like a horse.
The crew were deafened by the howling of the
    gales
and the timbers were shivered from the keel to the
    sails.
The ship was thrown about like a cork on the
    deep
but, down in the hold, Jonah was asleep.
(*Singing to nursery rhyme tune*)
*Rock-a-bye Jonah, in your bunk bed,*
*when you wake up, you may well be –*
(*The rhythm returns*)
Dead to the world, snoring like a drunk,
He slept through the storm in his tiny bunk
'til the Captain woke him up and said,

CAPTAIN    Get up and pray
that the Lord doesn't make this your last living
    day.

ALL    Up on deck Jonah faced the crew
who were desperate,

CREW MEMBER  We didn't have a clue!

ALL           Jonah was a fully paid-up landlubber;
              he started to wail and he started to blubber,

JONAH         This is all my fault for running off from the Lord.
              If you want to save yourselves then throw me
                  overboard.

CREW          What??? (*Pause*) Well, all right then . . .
              The waves crashed over, the ship began to sink
              so the crew grabbed Jonah and threw him in the
                  drink.

ALL           SPLASH!!! Sssssshhh . . .
              The waves died down, the storm-clouds cleared
              and, quietly bubbling, Jonah disappeared.
              The crew gave thanks, the ship sailed on,
              and the ordinary bloke from Joppa was

ALL           (*Singing to funeral march tune*)
              Gone gone g-gone, gone g-gone g-gone g-gone.
              Which would have been the end of this fishy tale
              if God hadn't sent along a great big whale.
              It swallowed him down – *gulp* – and the mighty
                  fish
              swam with Jonah, away from Tarshish.
              Jonah sloshed about in the cavernous bowel.

JONAH         Help, help, help!

ALL           Was his echoing echoing echoing howl.
              (*Pause*)

JONAH'S VOICE They play rugby in Wales, you know.

ACTOR         Yes, and they have leeks in Wales, too.

JONAH         LEAKS?! I'm going to drown!

ACTOR         Not that kind of leak, you clown . . .
              (*The rhythm returns*)

ALL           After three long days when time was a blur,
              There came a *heave!* and a *ho!* and a great, big
                  (*vomit noise*) Huurrr!

Jonah found himself face-down in the sand,
Vomited forth in an unknown land.
Watching the disappearing dorsal fin of 'er,
he realised he was lying on the beach at Nineveh!
Then the voice of God struck him like a harpoon
    – *aargh!*

GOD      You must do as you're told now you're out of that
     tuna!

ALL      The city wasn't pretty, it was full of bad folk;
a wave of fear seized our ordinary bloke,
but he picked himself up and he brushed himself
     down,
shook the sand from his sandals and went into
     town.
Soon he was lost in a crush of thieves,
of light-fingered losers with knives up their
     sleeves.

VARIOUS PEOPLE WITH ATTITUDE      I've got an idea – now this'll be
     fun –
let's plug tourists' nostrils with Smasher's new
     gun!
Let's hot-wire some camels and ram-raid some
     shops,
then throw bad eggs at Nineveh's cops!
(*Together*) *YEEAAH!!!*

ALL      There were pimps and pushers and scheisters and
     scruffs,
drugged up, drunk and rougher than rough –
Jonah lost his wallet, his watch

JONAH      And my rag!

ALL      And eight seconds later

JONAH      Enough is enough!

ALL      He stood right up in the noise and din of 'er

and preached in the market in the city of
    Nineveh.

JONAH      (*Extremely politely*) Ladies and gentlemen . . .
Er . . . Excuse me? Errm . . . Ah, ladies and gen-
tlemen?
(*Suddenly shouting them down with a huge voice*)
LADIES AND GENTLEMEN!

ALL      The crowd stood still.

JONAH      (*Regaining his evangelical politeness*)
The Lord has asked me to express his not incon-
siderable displeasure, and his willingness to exact
retribution at your, shall we say, reluctance to
comply whole-heartedly with his inestimable will.

CROWD      What?

JONAH      Stop doing evil, stop doing wrong,
start worshipping the Lord – you haven't got
    long –
because in forty days' time he wipes out this town
if he doesn't see your conduct turned around.

ALL      They still stood still, everyone silent,
Jonah was convinced they would soon turn
    violent,
but gradually a whisper rippled through the
    crowd
and together the people shouted aloud,

CROWD      We totally agree with what you're talking about.
You're absolutely right. Though you smell like a
    trout!
They threw off their silks and threw off their
    sashes,
and prayed and repented in sack-cloth and ashes.
(*They burst into a short stirring rendition of a
gospel number such as* 'O Happy Day')

| | |
|---|---|
| ALL | Jonah was introduced to the king of 'er |
| | and asked to repeat God's words to Nineveh. |
| | (*Jonah whispers into his ear*) |
| KING | Agreed! |
| ALL | Said the king |
| KING | We need to change our ways. |
| | God's word is true and it's here to stay. |
| ALL | The Lord was pleased with this resolution |
| | and changed his mind about retribution. |
| | Sorted! |
| | So an ordinary bloke changed the roughest of the rough |
| | from rock to gem, from ugly and tough |
| | to the best of the best, which may come as a shock. |
| | But remember – every diamond comes from an ordinary rock . . . |
| | So remember – every diamond comes from an ordinary rock! |

# In the Beginning . . .
## by Michael Peacock with Paul Burbridge

ADAM *a man confident in his knowledge of the natural world*
BARRY *his friend, suspicious of* ADAM's *confidence*

Riding Lights Roughshod companies often find themselves performing and leading discussions in secondary school PSE/RE
lessons. The old battleground of science versus religion is often
rolled out along the lines of little more than hearsay and a wide-
spread idea that the Christian perspective on life must be tosh,
because it gets everything very badly wrong at the start. In other
words, according to the 'science' of public perception, because
the very first chapter of the Bible is nonsense and the world was
not created by God, who therefore does not exist, there can be no
point in going any further with religion. Ridiculous maybe, but
it is surprising how many young people claim to believe this.
Roughshod companies, however, enjoy the cut and thrust of
classroom debate (at least that's what they tell us), so sketches
like this one have been written to provoke the discussion and
perhaps, through the humour, to explode some of the most
obvious misconceptions. In an area where some of the most
sophisticated minds in the world – both with a religious and a
non-religious outlook – still seek to discover the nature of
'How?' the universe began, it would be foolish for those of us

who are not astro-physicists to be very dogmatic. Frankly, *our* two pennyworth does not amount to very much. However, as people of faith, our expertise is in answering a different question. It is vital that we continue to present an answer to the question of 'Why?' the world began.

The situations in which ADAM and BARRY might have this conversation could be many and various – we leave that to your own invention. It is important that BARRY takes ADAM very seriously. . . .

# In the Beginning . . .

ADAM     I like to think sometimes.

BARRY     Do you?

ADAM     Let the mind wander into the uncharted territories of space and time.

BARRY     Wow.

ADAM     You see, the universe in which we live is something that we very often take for granted.

BARRY     I've never really thought about it.

ADAM     That's my point. For example – the stars in the sky. Do you know how many there are?

BARRY     No. How many?

ADAM     Well . . . there's a lot. You see, the universe is a fascinating place.

BARRY     Well, it's big, isn't it?

ADAM     It is infinite, Barry.

BARRY     That's even bigger, then. Someone must have had a lot of imagination.

ADAM     Imagination?

BARRY     Yeah. I mean, whoever invented all that different stuff – like zebras, for example.

ADAM     Zebras?

BARRY     I've always thought they were clever.

ADAM     What are you talking about? No one *invented* zebras. They're part of . . . part of . . . Mother Nature's natural evolutionary process.

BARRY     So Mother Nature invented them.

ADAM     No! They just . . . happened. You see, in the beginning, the universe was created by this huge explosion.

39

| | |
|---|---|
| BARRY | Blimey. How was that? |
| ADAM | Well, I don't know. I suppose it was an accident. |
| BARRY | An accident? I'll have to be more careful. I mean, it would be funny if I suddenly spilled a bottle of milk, and the next thing you know I've got giraffes and zebras running all over the kitchen. |
| ADAM | Barry, let me explain. In the beginning, there was nothing. |
| BARRY | Nothing? |
| ADAM | Not a sausage. You see, this was before recorded history. |
| BARRY | So how do you know? |
| ADAM | Eh? |
| BARRY | How do you know, if it was before recorded history? You could be guessing. |
| | (*Pause*) |
| ADAM | Can I get back to my point, Barry? |
| BARRY | OK. |
| ADAM | Fine. So then, all of a sudden, it exploded. |
| BARRY | What? Nothing exploded? |
| ADAM | Well, *something* obviously did. |
| BARRY | So what was that? |
| ADAM | Well, it was . . . nothing. |
| BARRY | How can nothing explode? |
| ADAM | Well, there must have been a bit of something. |
| BARRY | But you just said there was nothing. |
| ADAM | It was mostly nothing with a bit of something in it! |
| BARRY | And then someone blew it up? |
| ADAM | No! No one blew it up! |
| BARRY | So why did it explode? Was it having a bad day? 'Gosh, it's really boring here with all this nothing around – I think I'll just explode and see if a universe pops out.' |

ADAM        Barry, it was all done in a very controlled and
            scientific way.
            (*Pause*)
BARRY       I see.
ADAM        The Big Bang.
BARRY       (*Working it out*) Nothing – BANG! – Everything.
            Wow!
ADAM        Yes.
BARRY       And that's how we got zebras?
ADAM        Yes.
BARRY       It's pretty good, science.
ADAM        Yeah.
BARRY       (*With sudden inspiration*) Hey! You know that
            patio my mum wants me to do for her? Do you
            think I could use a bit of science on that? Nothing
            – BANG! – Patio!
            (*Adam starts to leave*)
ADAM        You could try, Barry.
BARRY       Yeah. 'Cos that would be really convenient,
            wouldn't it? (*Pursuing him offstage*) Save me
            getting all those paving stones from B&Q. 'Cos
            they're really heavy, especially with having to get
            loads of sand as well . . .
            (*They have gone*)

# Wonderful World
## by Paul Burbridge

STEWART *sixteen and into poetry and art*
KRYSTAL *sixteen and into physics and chemistry*

The theme of this little sketch is that the same world can be understood truthfully but differently by different people. Obvious – but invariably overlooked in an argument. For instance, are you the kind of person who would say, 'The plate is half empty', or are you naturally more optimistic and more likely to say, 'The plate is half full'? On which side of the great trans-Atlantic pronunciation dilemma are you on: 'You say "*tomato*" and I say "*tomato*"'? (This, of course, doesn't work quite so well on the page.) Left brain versus right brain. We all *know* that we look at the world in very different ways and we all understand the well-worn phrase, 'It depends where you're coming from . . .', but sometimes our understanding of any experience is impoverished because we refuse to entertain any perspective other than our own. This is especially significant when trying to awaken some understanding of mystery, faith and spiritual experience in those who take a reductionist 'this is nothing but . . .' attitude to the world. Hence the conversation here between these two teenagers.

# Wonderful World

*A young teenage couple are staring at a remarkable sunset. They have just met at a party.*

STEWART        Beautiful, isn't it? Really beautiful. When I look at a sunset like that, I think, 'That's really . . . (*Searching for an alternative*) . . . well, beautiful, really.' Like one of those paintings from Woolworth's, 'cept this one's all over the sky. 'God, 1994.' Makes you feel, well, you know . . . it's just such an amazing place to meet you. You look . . . well . . . beautiful.

KRYSTAL        Are you the bloke who does the turkey commercials?
               (*They both laugh*)

STEWART        Oh, yeah. Sorry. But that sky's just so . . . it's like poetry, isn't it? 'Romantic.' That's the word.

KRYSTAL        Steady.

STEWART        It is. The sun, the amazing colours, the clouds changing all the time, the evening flowers, the trees –

KRYSTAL        The pollution.

STEWART        (*Sighing*) Yeah.
               (*Pause*)
               What do you mean, 'the pollution'?

KRYSTAL        It's all the dust.

STEWART        What is?

KRYSTAL        That sunset.

STEWART        Eh?

KRYSTAL        That's all it is. As the sun gets lower, it shines through all the dust and fumes of the earth's atmosphere. The light gets bent by the interfering particles and separated into different colours. The filthier the atmosphere, the stronger the colours.

STEWART  Majestic, innit?

KRYSTAL  Just think what that sunset's doing to our lungs!

STEWART  No thanks. It might just destroy a teensy bit of the mystery.

KRYSTAL  There's no mystery up there. We even *made* a sunset at school once in science – by projecting white light through a fishtank full of photographic fixative and hydrochloric acid.

STEWART  Sounds exciting.

KRYSTAL  It was quite.

STEWART  Especially for the fish.
(*Pause*)
Do you fancy going out on Saturday?

KRYSTAL  Yeah, OK.

STEWART  Great. What's your name?

KRYSTAL  Krystal.

STEWART  That's nice. What, like, er . . .?

KRYSTAL  The transparent mineral with the perfect molecular structure?

STEWART  I was going to say 'sherry glasses'.

KRYSTAL  What's yours?

STEWART  Stew. Doesn't sound very scientific, does it? But kind of rich and tasty.

KRYSTAL  Stew.

STEWART  Stewart Carmichael, yeah. My science teacher told me it was an anagram of 'chemical waste'. I never liked science much.

| | |
|---|---|
| KRYSTAL | What *do* you like, then? |
| STEWART | Poetry. Music. Sunsets. |
| KRYSTAL | Rainbows? |
| STEWART | Yeah! Big fan of rainbows! They make you feel all hopeful after the storm clouds disappear. (*Pause*) Actually, they probably don't make you feel that at all, do they? |
| KRYSTAL | Not really. I just think about spherical droplets splitting the visible part of electro-solar radiation into its component frequencies. |
| STEWART | You know, we should get on like a house on fire! |
| KRYSTAL | What do you mean? |
| STEWART | Well, we don't exactly live on the same planet, do we? So there'll be lots to talk about. If we can understand one another. The question you should be asking yourself is, 'What does the rainbow *mean*?' And don't start all that spherical droplets business again. |
| KRYSTAL | It doesn't have to *mean* anything. (*She gives him a quick kiss*) |
| STEWART | So what does that mean, then? |
| KRYSTAL | I'll see you Saturday. |
| STEWART | Just that? Nothing noble, deep and eternal, stirring the heart? |
| KRYSTAL | Well, possibly a chemical upsurge of unclassifiable feeling, resulting in a mutual transmission of microbes and bacteria. |
| STEWART | Euurgh! What a brave, exciting world you must live in, eh? (*Pause*) Do you want to transmit again? Or shall we just walk off now into the twisted solar rays and inhale a few more interfering particles? |

KRYSTAL    You keep your hands to yourself. I'll see you on
           Saturday.
           (*She leaves*)
STEWART    Are you going already?
           (*Calling after her*)
           There's still a bit of fading atmospheric filth to
           look at!
           (*Pause*)
           Don't I even get a goodnight bacteria?!

# Life! Wassitallabout?
### by Paul Burbridge, Bridget Foreman, Andrew Harrison and Cathy Wardle

A GROUP OF BOYS AND GIRLS, *a minimum of two of each, working out in the gym*

Done with impressive energy and gusto, this sketch is a great ensemble piece. It has proved a surefire success in difficult situations where the performers need to grab the attention of a restless or perhaps a sceptical audience. Roughshod have often started this sketch by rushing on stage and shouting the title *Life! Wassitallabout?* extremely loudly, before beginning a vigorous (though not too fast) physical routine to accompany the text. The group which is not speaking at any point vocalise a rhythm to underscore the words of the other group. Choreographing the whole sketch takes patience and great discipline from everybody, but the results are usually extremely entertaining.

# Life! Wassitallabout?

*Groups of young men and women are working out in the gym. They work in synchronised pairs (at the very least) and illustrate their text with appropriate but simple actions. They establish a sustainable rhythm which provides a solid basis for the words and the actions. The only variation to this will come towards the end of the sketch, as the increasing age of the 'characters' demands a slower pace in keeping with their advancing decrepitude.*

BOYS      Down the gym, keep in trim,
work that body, keep it slim.
In the sauna, things get hot.
I cough a lot. So what?

GIRLS      Monday morning, up with the lark,
off to work as a filing clerk.
Tuesday night, me an' Louise
watch a video and eat Chinese.
Work on Wednesday's always fun –
the manager comes to pinch my bum!
(*They retire giggling as the boys come forward again*)

BOYS      Doing weights with me mates,
earn good money working 'lates'.
Watch TV, take Ecstasy;
my head feels funny but I'm really free
I think, I think, I think, I think . . .

GIRLS      Go to aerobics Thursday night,
work that body, keep it tight.
Friday night it's party time!
(*One of them throws up in the toilet*)

Chicken madras and a lager and lime.
Saturday night I'm out with Jim.
I think he'll ask me to marry him.

BOYS     Oi, Rick! I've got this chick!
She looks so good but she's really thick.
She's quite a find – just my kind –
but I can't seem to get no peace of mind.

GIRLS     A few years on, get the kids to school,
my cozzie bulges at the swimming pool.
Want some razzle, fancy the pub;
Jim drags me down the working men's club.
Thursday's still aerobics day –
keeping in shape, Jim likes me that way.

BOYS     Got a house, got a car, got a private bar,
got a yacht, got a villa in Mar-bay-yah.
I'm older now and my belly's gone fat.
Starting to worry about looking a prat.

GIRLS     Doing the housework takes me hours.
Jim can't afford to buy me flowers.
Saturday's a family day,
But Nintendo's all we play.
It's doing my head in, almost dead,
'School in the morning, so early to bed!'

BOYS     We're having a bash, no shortage of cash,
but the music's all strange and I've got a bad rash.
(*Singing drunkenly*) '*I'm a pink toothbrush and
you're a pink toothbrush . . .*'

GIRLS     I'm older now, got dodgy knees,
and walking too far makes me wheeze.
Doctor tells me I'm pretty sick.
Must be the fags – better give up quick.

BOYS     We're keeping our youth by avoiding the truth,
laugh when the kids call us long in the tooth.

| | |
|---|---|
| GIRLS | Meals on Wheels brings me dinner. |
| | I don't know why but I'm getting thinner. |
| | Bingo night! I go with Pru. |
| | Now Jim's gone I need things to do. |
| BOYS | Life is full of small adventures |
| | like searching for each other's dentures. |
| | Now I'm keeping much, much trimmer |
| | just by walking with my zimmer. |
| GIRLS | My friends are photos on the wall, |
| | I'm in all day but no one calls. |
| BOYS | Well I made it to the top of the family tree. |
| | Never thought I'd be an OAP. |
| GIRLS | This morning I got a dizzy spell, |
| | better sit down – I don't feel well. |
| BOYS | My sight's not good and my hearing's poor |
| ALL | And I'm always afraid to answer the door. |
| | (*They create the SFX*) KNOCK, KNOCK, KNOCK! |
| | (*All look look towards the door, shaking with fear.* *They suddenly collapse with heart failure*) |
| | (*SFX of a cardiac machine turning itself off*) |
| | **BIP, BIP, BIP, BEEEEEEP** |

# Porter's Prodigal
## by Nigel Forde

REPORTER *from a local newspaper*
FRANK *42, an unemployed builder*
GILLIAN *16, his daughter*
SIMON *19, his son*

Jesus' story of the son who was 'lost' and then welcomed back into the family by an overjoyed father is perhaps the most famous story of all time. It is certainly the one that Christian preachers are most grateful for when trying to expound the heart of the gospel. Its cutting edge is in its emotional power and the way in which the father's forgiving reaction is a challenge to our accepted understanding of justice. To feel its depth, the audience has to be 'right there', identifying with and involved in the story. Because much of our work has taken us into areas of society where people's experience of family security is slight and living conditions are harsh, we wanted to find an atmosphere for Jesus' story which would be worlds away from some grinning, cereal-packet notion of happy family life to which the prodigal would return. We came up with this version, not to patronise the context it portrays but rather to celebrate the honesty of feeling and the depth of love, tested by hardship, which can be found there.

# Porter's Prodigal

THE PORTERS *are a single-parent family, living in a depressing tower-block flat. The incidents which the sketch describes have already happened. The audience is discovering them as if reading about them in the local newspaper and so the sketch employs various documentary techniques such as reported speech, journalistic comment, 'freeze-frame photographs' with captions and headlines. To begin with, as the story starts to unfold, each character addresses the audience directly, prompted by the questions of the* REPORTER. *Later, as the action progresses, the sequences are fully dramatised.*

REPORTER    (*Quoting tabloid headlines*) Horror Homes in Midnight Mayhem! Police Probe Prodigal!
            For the fourth time in as many months, police were called out to the notorious Mandela Place and the tower-block known to locals as Nelson's Column. Panic-stricken residents reported shouts and screams and even smoke pouring from the kitchen window of number 37, the home of –

FRANK       Frank Porter, forty-two,

REPORTER    and his two children. Our crime correspondent was on the spot. Frank Porter, an unemployed builder, spoke grimly of life on the estate.

FRANK       Planners' Paradise, they called it in the sixties. It was called Douglas Bader Close then. Yeah, well they changed the name, but that's all that *has* changed. Fifty people in this block, eight of them have got jobs. Pat, my wife – well, it was all too

57

|  |  |
|---|---|
|  | much for her which, well, it makes it harder for me in lots of ways. Two kids. They need more than I can ever give them. |
| REPORTER | One of those two kids is . . . |
| GILLIAN | Gillian, sixteen, |
| REPORTER | but streetwise beyond her years. She has just started secretarial college. |
| GILLIAN | It might be a way out. Anything'd be better than this place. I don't blame Dad, he does his best. I s'pose it annoys me that he's always, like, trying to look on the bright side, only there isn't a bright side. It's my brother, Simon – I could kill him sometimes. |
| FRANK | You can't give up, can you? Not when you've got kids. Where there's life, there's hope. I got a bit of money put away in the desk – don't trust banks – and when we've got enough, me and my lad, we're going into business together. You can't save much on the dole, but give it time. |
| REPORTER | Time, though, for nineteen-year-old Simon, seems to be running out. |
| SIMON | This job thing, right? It won't work. He's like a kid on Christmas Eve. Tomorrow everything's going to be wonderful. Even if some old git in a white beard *does* come down the chimney, the most we'll get out of it is a pile of soot and a smashed-up bird's nest. Doing my head in. Soon as I can, I'm off. |
| REPORTER | Two years ago, all the buildings on this estate were scheduled for demolition within six months. A council spokesman admitted that the plan had never been thrown out but, at present, there wasn't enough in the budget to fund any redevelopment. |

| | |
|---|---|
| GILLIAN | You take your life in your hands walking up the stairs. It's an adventure playground for alcos and druggies. |
| SIMON | The pub's not much to write home about. Wouldn't go in at weekends, mind; but during the week – well, there's nothing else to do. |
| GILLIAN | You seen *The Bill*, right? You seen *Cracker*? *Prime thingy*? Yeah, well, it's like that round here. |
| FRANK | There's a bit of a garden down there. Not exactly Hyde Park, but it's something. Bit of green. Brown usually, and a . . . well, I don't know what it is, really. Mahonia? Green. Sharp. |
| SIMON | In the corner there's swings. Well, *a* swing, and a few dangling chains. There's usually a fight there at least once a night. You walk past in the morning, the ground's all covered with needles. |
| GILLIAN | All the phone boxes have been smashed and they stink of pee. There's one shop, a newsagents. Used to be run by Mr Chak. That's not his actual name, it's short for . . . something longer. He got mugged for ten Mars Bars by three twelve-year-olds. Now he can't walk. |
| REPORTER | Breaches of peace are far from unusual on this estate but, as Gillian explained, last night's was something out of the ordinary. |
| GILLIAN | You can't do anything with Simon around. He's such a slob. I've got to get to work if he hasn't. There's all his friends lying all over the floor and you don't have to be a genius to bet they've been drinking lager. The stink! |
| SIMON | (*Talking to her for the first time*) You're not the only one in this house, you know. |
| GILLIAN | Don't I know it! |

| | |
|---|---|
| FRANK | Come on, that'll do! |
| GILLIAN | I'm the only one who's earning any money. You realise it's my grant you're drinking away. |
| SIMON | They bring their own cans. You should make sure of your facts. |
| FRANK | Look, calm down, both of you! |
| GILLIAN | It's no wonder Mum couldn't stand it any more! |
| SIMON | Yeah, well she's not the only one! |
| FRANK | That'll *do*! Simon – clean this place up. Gillian, you get off. |
| SIMON | (*Back to the audience*) That was it! Same row as we'd had day after day, but that was the last one as far as I was concerned. I went to the drawer in the big desk and I took half the money we'd put away for the business: Porter and Son Ltd. Well, it was my money, that's how I looked at it, and I took half. I was only taking what was mine. Anyway, I left a note. Didn't say much. And I went. <br> (*Pause*) |
| FRANK | Where is he? Gillian, where is he? What's he done? |
| GILLIAN | Good riddance. |
| FRANK | The money! All that money! Why? What have I done? |
| GILLIAN | He's done it all, not you. He's gone. Let him go, Dad. |
| FRANK | He's gone! He's gone! |
| SIMON | I went north. Places I'd only heard of on maps. Newark, Doncaster, York, Durham, Retford – I just counted seven stops and got off. Found some guys to have a drink with. It's not difficult when you're flush. We had a laugh, few drinks. Hey, not all girls are like Gillian, I can tell you! |
| GILLIAN | Dad? Are you all right? |

| | |
|---|---|
| FRANK | Me? Yeah, don't you worry. |
| GILLIAN | You been out today? |
| FRANK | Um, yeah . . . I went out for a bit. |
| GILLIAN | I'm going to my evening class. |
| FRANK | That's right. |
| GILLIAN | Shall I get you something to eat before I go? |
| FRANK | No, you're all right. |
| GILLIAN | Wouldn't you like that? |
| FRANK | I had something earlier. |
| GILLLIAN | Right. Well, I'll see you soon. |
| FRANK | Yeah, go careful. Don't be late. Gillian, don't be late! |
| GILLIAN | Bye. |
| SIMON | How often does it happen, eh? You have this dream. You're there. It's happening. A huge, soaring bungy-jump into everything you ever wanted. And then . . . then there's just a twitch, a little shudder. It's nothing. But it is. And the blue water is suddenly black, and the sand is a solid rockface and the smiling dolphins, the gentle dolphins are sharks; and no one hears you screaming, 'Stop!' and you're going to hit it and nothing can help you. Down and down and the darkness is closing over you and the nightmare has come. And it says 'Go on! Go on!' and I can't go on, I've got to . . . I've got to go back. But I can't go back. I *can't*. Not back to . . . I can't. Can I? |
| FRANK | Doorbell rang. Gill must've forgotten her keys. |
| GILLIAN | Forgot me keys. Sorry. |
| FRANK | I was looking over her shoulder. |
| GILLIAN | Dad? You all right? You've gone white. |
| FRANK | So it was almost dark. But I knew it was him. Coming across the square, just as if nothing had |

|  | happened. You think I wouldn't recognise my boy? You keep coming! You keep coming, boy! |
|---|---|
| GILLIAN | I dropped my things in the hall. I couldn't believe what I was seeing. |
| FRANK | (*His voice is full of suppressed emotion, so that it is impossible to judge whether his mood is determination or anger*) Don't you veer one inch off that path, boy! I want you here! |
| SIMON | I couldn't see his face, but it was the right door. I had to run or I'd have turned back. And then he started to run too. |
| FRANK | Keep coming, boy! Keep coming! |
| SIMON | He was shouting something and his arms were flailing in the air; and I shouted, I don't know what I shouted and my face was wet and my throat was throbbing. |
|  | (*Frank and Simon are both talking and shouting simultaneously as they 'run' towards the audience*) |
| FRANK | I'm coming to get you, boy! I've been waiting for this; I've had dreams too, and this is what I've dreamt of. If you change your mind now. You let me have my turn. Come on! You come here! |
| SIMON | Look at his face! It's wild! Whatever he does, I've deserved it. I can't run away again. I didn't mean it, Dad – I didn't know. Don't look like that! I've come home! I'm sorry, I'm sorry! |
|  | (*At the last moment they suddenly turn and face each other. For a second, it looks as if Frank is going to smash Simon. They crash into each other's arms with a great howl. They stand there clasped to each other, freeze a second, then pose with their arms around each other's shoulders for the picture which will appear in the paper*) |

| | |
|---|---|
| REPORTER | Hold it. |
| BOTH | (*Giving us the caption*) 'I was over the moon.' |
| GILLLIAN | Well, that's one moon this cow isn't going to jump over. |
| FRANK | (*Full of a sparkle which we haven't seen before*) Gillian, go and get those spare ribs out of Mrs Chapman's freezer. |
| GILLIAN | Me? |
| FRANK | We're having a party. Knock on the wall, Simon, then go and get your old mates. And bring back some pizzas and some cans. |
| SIMON | (*How can he say this?*) I haven't got any money. |
| | (*They stare at each other for a second, and then roar with laughter*) |
| FRANK | (*Giving him money*) Here! |
| | (*Freeze for another flash photo*) |
| SIMON | I couldn't stop laughing. All through the evening. |
| FRANK | We never had such a party! |
| GILLIAN | (*Sulking*) And you couldn't move for sweaty bodies and cheesy grins. |
| FRANK | Some people brought Chinese, some brought curry – there were bottles everywhere. |
| SIMON | And the old ghetto blaster going – boom boom boom boom. Few tunes. Yeah! |
| GILLIAN | That's it, is it? That's life, eh? |
| | (*Another photo: Gillian looking suitably askance while Frank and Simon are full of delight*) |
| SIMON | She's not pleased. Boyfriend problems. |
| FRANK | The best thing was – |
| | (*There is a loud 'bang!' behind them, followed by the sounds of dogs barking, neighbours shouting, police sirens*) |

|  | I thought they'd started the demolition without telling anybody. |
|---|---|
| SIMON | Dirty great explosion! Course, the old bill arrived, didn't they? Blue uniforms everywhere. |
| FRANK | (*Turns and shouts to the neighbours*) All right, shut up! |
| SIMON | Some genius had put nine pizzas in the microwave.<br>(*Pointing out the mess all over the walls*) |
| FRANK | Cheese. |
| SIMON | Tomato. |
| FRANK | Anchovies. |
| GILLIAN | (*Offering some*) Sultanas. |
| FRANK | Sultanas? (*He looks more closely into her hand*) You don't get sultanas in . . . blimey . . . |
| ALL | The rabbit hutch!<br>(*Freeze as the final camera flash goes off*) |

# Travellers' Fare
## by Paul Burbridge
## (updated from *The Good Punk Rocker* by Paul Burbridge and Murray Watts)

NARRATOR
CHORUS *anything from four to fifteen actors*

Those who know a little about the work of Riding Lights Theatre Company will probably have heard of *The Parable of the Good Punk Rocker* which formed a staple part of the company's initial repertoire in 1977 and was published in our first book *Time to Act* in 1979. They may also, quite understandably, have cursed the day we were born, such has been the popularity of this sketch and the countless performances of it which have been given throughout the world, with vastly varying attention to quality, no doubt. 'Theatrical icon of its time' or 'Tiresome piece of rubbish'? – it is not for us to judge, but we can alleviate some of the pain by offering an alternative version here which is not locked up in such a brief cultural time zone . . . or just think of it as a cover version of our own song.

# Travellers' Fare

*Led by the* NARRATOR, THE CHORUS *assemble on stage like passengers waiting on a railway platform. After various train announcements in various European languages, they 'board' the Eurostar connection to London where this is indicated in the script. Over the years we have experimented with different ways of creating the sounds and rhythms of the train which underscore the whole piece: we have used drumming from offstage, actors onstage playing complementary percussion instruments and actors creating vocal effects or beating out rhythms on their knees. The choice is yours, but keeping the sound and movement of the train going is crucial to the coherence of the sketch.*

| | |
|---|---|
| ALL | (*Snatches of rail platform announcements in various European languages*) |
| VOICE | Welcome to Eurostar! Bitte einsteigen und Türen schliessen. |
| NARRATOR | There was a train on its way to London from Munich and Bonn<br>(*A train rhythm is established*) |
| ALL | Munich and Bonn<br>Munich and Bonn<br>Munich and Bonn |
| NARRATOR | Via Paris and somewhere in Kent |
| ALL | somewhere in Kent<br>somewhere in Kent<br>somewhere in Kent |
| NARRATOR | The train was full of members of the British National Front Party. |
| ALL | (*Singing raucously*) Rule Britannia! Britannia |

rules the waves. Britons never, never, never shall be slaves!

NARRATOR    And supporters of England's football team . . .
(*There is a brief whispered consultation among the actors as to how to portray these people*)

ALL    (*Singing raucously*) Rule Britannia! Britannia rules the waves.
(*Clapping rhythm*) Cha! Cha! Cha-cha-cha! Cha-cha-cha-cha! Cha-cha!

NARRATOR    Who had just been entertained by another goal-less draw.

ALL    Boo! Whaadaaloadaarubbish!

NARRATOR    So, to cheer themselves up, they had a fight.
(*Stylised violence with sound effects*)
Which made them feel much better.
(*They all feel much better as they nurse their re-arranged faces*)

FANS    I feel great!

NARRATOR    Except for one National Front activist who was stabbed in the neck and left half dead.

ALL    (*Singing triumphantly*) You'll never walk again, a-a-gain!

NARRATOR    Now on that train was a Buddhist surgeon from Amsterdam, who felt disturbed by the situation.

SURGEON    Zis iss deeply uncivilisink.

NARRATOR    So he hid in the toilette and meditated.
(*Sound effect of electronic door sliding shut. The Dutch surgeon sits and starts snorting coke*)
Also on that train was an animal rights campaigner from Surrey, protesting in Europe about the slaughter of dumb animals.

PROTESTER    (*Deeply green-wellied*) I really care about the cows! I really care about the little cows!

NARRATOR    She stepped over the wounded man on her way to the buffet for a salad sandwich.

(*She does so*)

Also on that train was Mr Deepak Patel, an Asian businessman from Leicester, who was on his way back from a conference in Switzerland.

ALL    (*Severally*) He saw the man,

his shaven head,

his ugly face,

his boots and Union Jack.

He raised his fist . . .

(*All raise their fists, as if to strike the wounded man*)

NARRATOR    And grabbed the emergency cord.

(*SFX: train screeching to a halt*)

He phoned for help

(*SFX: mobile phone followed by approaching ambulance*)

Left the man 500 Euros to cover his medical treatment

(*SFX: paper money*)

And saw him onto the ambulance.

(*SFX: ambulance door, siren disappearing*)

SURGEON    Zis iss deeply civilisink.

NARRATOR    Now, where Mr Patel lived, Asian homes were attacked . . .

NARRATOR    His kids got beaten up . . .

ALL    (*Sing 'Rule Britannia'*)

NARRATOR    But there were plenty of doctors . . .

(*SFX: hospitals*)

And social activists . . .

ALL    What do we want?

THE RIGHT TO WORK!
When do we want it?
NOW!

ONE VOICE     (*Slightly behind the others*) Thursday!

NARRATOR     But when it came to the (*SFX: crunch*)
Who was prepared to cross cultural barriers, show solidarity with the oppressed and promote the bond of social cohesion within the heart of the European community?
(*Pause*)

VOICE     Yer wot?

NARRATOR     Who helped the thug?

VOICE 2     . . . the one who was brave enough to care for his enemy?

NARRATOR     Who showed love, love, love, love.
Jesus said, Go! And do the same.

ALL     Love, love, love your neighbour.
Love, love, love your neighbour.
(*Repeat and fade out to the train rhythm*)

# Bully for You
## by Nigel Forde

DIANA 1 *a school bully*
DIANA 2 *the voice of her thoughts*
SALLY 1 *a girl at the same school*
SALLY 2 *the voice of her thoughts*

This sketch was one response to many requests from teachers and pupils for Roughshod companies to tackle the perennial problem of bullying at school. Initially we approached it through a series of repeated improvisations with the actors, as we tried not only to get underneath the skin of the problem ourselves, but also to give the audience a way of getting under its skin too. This led to the device of having a second actor shadowing each of the main characters, allowing the audience to hear the thoughts behind the words; to hear the thoughts and therefore to understand some of the motives and secret fears which control both the bullied and the bully in these situations.

# Bully for You

*Two schoolgirls meet in the changing rooms. Each girl is shadowed by her own 'alter ego' – another actor (perhaps wearing a mask) who speaks the thoughts which lie beneath the dialogue. These 'alter egos' stay close behind their 'subjects' and occasionally address each other directly.*

| | |
|---|---|
| DIANA 1 | Oi! You! I'm talking to you! |
| *DIANA 2* | *Go on, say it.* |
| DIANA 1 | Oi! Fatty Spice! |
| *SALLY 2* | *Don't call me that.* |
| DIANA 1 | Well? |
| SALLY 1 | What? |
| DIANA 1 | You know 'what'. Come on, where is it? Where. Is. It? |
| *SALLY 2* | *Make a stand? Or give in?* |
| SALLY 1 | Look, I haven't got it. I can't . . . I haven't got it. |
| DIANA 1 | You haven't got it? |
| *DIANA 2* | *Careful! Nothing physical; you might lose. Keep it verbal.* |
| DIANA 1 | Oh dear! That was very clever of Spotty Spice, wasn't it? Well! Isn't she a glutton for punishment? |
| *SALLY 2* | *Don't say anything. The bell's going to go in a minute.* |
| DIANA 1 | Correct me if I'm wrong, but that makes it Monday, Tuesday and Wednesday you owe me for. That's a lot of money. |
| SALLY 1 | Haven't got any money. |

73

| | |
|---|---|
| *DIANA 2* | *She's not going to pay. The little cow isn't going to pay. She's going to call our bluff.* |
| **DIANA 1** | So what are you going to do about it? |
| *DIANA 2* | *We'll never get that much out of her.* |
| **SALLY 1** | Dunno. |
| **DIANA 1** | (*Mocking*) Dunno! |
| *SALLY 2* | *That's the way. Play for time. She's never actually done anything. Yet.* |
| *DIANA 2* | *You can't actually do anything. She could flatten you. Keep it mental.* |
| **DIANA 1** | No brain, no hope, no future – Michelin Spice. |
| *SALLY 2* | *What if someone comes? I don't want anyone to see this.* |
| *DIANA 2* | *What if someone comes? I don't want anyone to see this.* |
| *SALLY 2* | (*Addressing* DIANA *2*) *Why do you do it, then? What's it all about?* |
| *DIANA 2* | (*Responding to this*) *Why do you put up with it?* |
| *SALLY 2* | *Who could we tell?* |
| *DIANA 2* | *Who can we talk to?* |
| *SALLY 2* | *Talk to? You don't talk to us. You sneer, you insult, you threaten. You don't call that talking?* |
| *DIANA 2* | *Because you've got no respect. You don't respond. You just stand there.* |
| *SALLY 2* | *You want us to like you?* |
| *DIANA 2* | *Shut up. We don't care! We're all right!* |
| **DIANA 1** | I'll tell you what I'll do. |
| **SALLY 1** | What? |
| **DIANA 1** | You owe me £1.20, right? |
| **SALLY 1** | Only 'cos you say I do. |
| **DIANA 1** | So, you bring me your *Backstreet Boys* CD. |
| **SALLY 1** | No! |
| **DIANA 1** | And we might let it go for this week. |

| | |
|---|---|
| SALLY 1 | It was a birthday present. |
| DIANA 1 | So? |
| *DIANA 2* | *So she might have to explain where it's gone. And why.* |
| DIANA 1 | If it was a present, you can do what you like with it. Right? Right?? |
| SALLY 1 | They'll think I didn't like it. |
| *DIANA 2* | *A present? Who from?* |
| *SALLY 2* | *From our parents. They can't afford it. Not really. But they bought it.* |
| *DIANA 2* | *Well, we want a present, all right? We want a present! We want someone to give us a present too, and . . . and no one does. Do they? No. So we'll have this one.* |
| *SALLY 2* | *You really like spoiling things, don't you?* |
| *DIANA 2* | *Everything's spoiled! You see what it's like!* |
| SALLY 1 | You haven't got a CD player. |
| DIANA 1 | Who says? Who says I haven't got a CD player? |
| SALLY 1 | Dunno. |
| DIANA 1 | I'm getting one for Christmas. I'm always getting presents. Whatever I ask for. I'm getting a CD player and a computer and a . . . whatever I want. I only have to ask for it. |
| SALLY 1 | You're getting a computer? |
| DIANA 1 | Yeah. |
| *SALLY 2* | *Go on, say it. You can't lose anything.* |
| SALLY 1 | Can I have a go on it? |
| *DIANA 2* | *We'd have someone we could . . . I mean . . . like a friend . . . only, we're not going to get a computer. Are we?* |
| | (DIANA 1 *and* SALLY 1 *look at each other for a moment, then any possibility of friendship fades*) |
| DIANA 1 | No! You'd break it, you're so fat. |

(DIANA 1 *and* DIANA 2 *go, leaving* SALLY 1 *and* SALLY 2 *alone*)

SALLY 2   *What are we going to do? (Silence) We can't go on like this. We'll have to do something.*

(SALLY 1 *sees another child offstage. Shall she? Shan't she?*)

SALLY 1   Oi! You! I'm talking to you. (*School bell*) Just stay where you are. You got your dinner money? . . . (*They both go*)

# Rhubarb Rhubarb
## by Paul Burbridge with Murray Watts

A COMPANY OF ACTORS; *the minimum is four. The company will need to identify individuals to play* A FOREMAN *on a building site and* TERRY WOGAN. *The facility to reproduce various international accents is also required.*

This is one of those sketches which almost requires to be seen, rather than read, in the first instance. The combination of vegetables, gibberish, building, the United Nations and national songs may seem fatally eccentric. In which case, you will have to take our word for the fact that, once all the physical choreography and all the 'clips' of the songs are in place, it works tremendously well with an audience – certainly a British audience, on whom the irony of a link between the Tower of Babel and the Eurovision Song Contest will not be wasted.

# Rhubarb Rhubarb

*The company forms up in two lines and begins to jog on the spot facing the audience. They are peasants on their way to work.*

| | |
|---|---|
| ALL | In the days of old when men were bold<br>They built a tower called Babel. |
| ONE | Now the whole earth had one language and few words<br>Rhubarb, rhubarb, rhubarb and rhubarb.<br>(*Pause*)<br>A form of ancient Rhubarbaritic which was extremely easy to learn.<br>(*Running U.S. Marines*) |
| TWO | The whole human race worked happily together.<br>(*They mime a building site*) |
| THREE | They sang and they worked and they built a tower.<br>It would reach to heaven – a monument to human pride! |
| ALL | (*Saluting the tower*) Rhubarb! Rhubarb! Rhubarb!<br>(*They form a noble statue of heroic workers*) |
| FOUR | They were one people, with one language, and one ambition:<br>To be like God!<br>(*Freeze. They sing a stirring Eastern European working song and then they begin again to build the tower higher and higher, using their one word 'rhubarb' as they pass each brick from person to person*) |

ONE

They built up and up and up
Until something strange began to happen . . .
(*Without warning a new vegetable is introduced into the sequence by one actor*)
Rhubarb, rhubarb, rhubarb, turnip.
(*Pause*)
(*They pretend they haven't heard and continue building until it happens again. This time from another actor with an Irish accent*)
Rhubarb, rhubarb, rhubarb, rhubarb, potato, potato, potato.
(*Silence. The foreman approaches the Irish person menacingly*)

FOREMAN

Rhubarb, rhubarb, rhubarb, rhubarb, 'potato', rhubarb?

TWO

(*Deaf*) 'Potato?'

FOREMAN

(*Repeating the accusation*) Rhubarb, rhubarb, rhubarb, rhubarb, 'potato', rhubarb!
(*The others are drawn into the argument that develops. The word rhubarb gradually disappears and individual national fruit and veg emerge until all are hysterically chanting their own, fighting for control of the tower, which collapses*)

THREE

They were scattered over the face of the earth.
Nation opposed nation.

FOUR

They continued to build alone . . .
(*The actors now build individually, illustrating their different edifices with physical actions*)

ALL
(*severally*)

Temples
Pyramids
Castles
Citadels
Skyscrapers

|         | Theme parks |
|---------|-------------|
|         | Space stations |
|         | The Millennium Dome! |
| ONE     | And they protected their interests with |
| ALL     | Clubs |
| *(together)* | Spears |
|         | Guns |
|         | Bazookas |
|         | Missiles |
|         | Chemicals |
|         | Atom bombs |
|         | Nuclear warheads. |

ONE        To avert disaster they made futile attempts at peaceful co-existence:

ALL        Treaties, Alliances, Diplomats, Rounds of talks, NATO, the European Union, the United Nations!
*(Everyone on headsets jabbering away, unable to understand a thing – mounting frustration)*

ONE        Finally, on the eve of the Third World War, in desperation they organised . . .

ALL        THE EUROVISION SONG CONTEST!!!
*(The actor who espoused potatoes sings a mournful Irish ballad. Potato is the only lyric)*
*(Applause)*

ONE        These are the results of the Maltese jury.

TWO        L'Irlande, douze points.

WOGAN      Hold onto your hats, now, here comes Turkey.
*(Another performance, this time a very intense emotionally charged piece, accompanied by dramatic dance movements. Olives are clearly the sole subject)*
*(Applause)*

TWO           Turkie, one point.

THREE         Deez are de votings of dee Norwegian – (*Click*)

WOGAN         Turkey, still only one point. But keep your fingers
              crossed now for the UK.
              (*A black soul number, strongly featuring mangoes
              and pineapples*)
              (*Applause*)

ONE           Thank you, London, and good night.

TWO           Way out in front at this stage, it's Portugal!

WOGAN         Now an upbeat little number from Poland. He's a
              cheery chappie . . .
              (*The song of the Warsaw turnip gatherers – some-
              what sent up by the backing group. The word
              'turnip' is the only lyric. Eventually the Polish
              singer stops and glares at his backing group who
              are sniggering*)

POLAND        Are you making fun of my culture?
              (*Pause. The backing group gives him various guilty
              apologies and encouragements to continue. The
              singer is deeply offended*)
              You make fun of my grandmother? She wrote
              this song in the time of the turnip famine. In
              Warsaw. Many people die!
              (*He leaves the stage, followed by the rest of the
              company remonstrating and trying to get him to
              cheer up. There is a brief struggle offstage, ending
              with the sound of a solid thump to someone's
              person and then sudden silence*)

FOUR          World peace . . . (*Embarrassed laugh*) . . . nul
              point!

# Zacchaeus – A Short Story
## by Bridget Foreman

A COMPANY OF ACTORS; *a group of disgruntled citizens from Jericho. They tell the story by dividing the lines between them and illustrating the text with physical action. One actor plays* ZACCHAEUS *throughout.*

Another classic group narration of a famous biblical story. It will take both time and ingenuity to rehearse the various elements which this sketch requires. The director's first job is to help the whole group understand how to deliver the rhythm of each line and then, once that has been established throughout, to share the lines appropriately between the actors so that minor characters can emerge here and there within the crowd – a chef, a farmer, a mother and child, Jesus, various factory workers, etc. This sharing out of the text needs to be done in conjunction with working out the illustrative actions for each 'scene' or section within the story.

To help you deliver the rhythm within the text (though you may wish to use your own variations to this), generally the rule is four beats to each line. In other words, you need to find the four stressed syllables that keep the whole rhythm tied down to a steady 'BOM-ching, BOM-ching, BOM-ching, BOM-ching'. For instance, the first two lines:

It was **just** another **Fri**day in **Jer**i-**cho**
**Ev**eryone at **work** – just an **hour** to **go** . . .

Once the basic rhythm has been established, it can be fun to break the rule occasionally for dramatic emphasis. Even as written, it is intended that the group should break rhythm to shout the name 'Zacchaeus!' (or in one instance 'Jesus!') at certain moments. This provides an opportunity to introduce a different rhythm in the following section for the sake of variety. We have found that using two contrasting rhythms within the piece works well. Roughshod has rehearsed this in various styles, in one instance using a wash-tub bass, hand-held percussion instruments and a dustbin as a drum – the actors providing their own rhythmic underscore for the words and actions. Be bold, be creative . . . but keep the words CLEAR!

# Zacchaeus – A Short Story

It was just another Friday in Jericho,
Everyone at work – just an hour to go.
The factory machines were winding down for the
day,
The hotel chef had made his final brulée,
And down on the farm, the hired hand
Had ploughed the last furrow in the farmer's land.
Friday was over! The weekend had come!
But for one person work hadn't yet begun.
Zacchaeus!
Zacc was the local collector of taxes.
He hoarded the money in boxes and sacks. His
Sole aim in life was to add to his stash,
His house – it was rumoured – was crammed full
of cash.
Every cupboard and drawer, every cranny and
nook
Was stuffed to the brim with the money he took.
Zacchaeus created a steep tax on working,
But if you were jobless, he'd tax you for shirking.
If you retired, he'd tax you for leaving,
He'd tax you for eating, or sleeping, or breathing.
Somebody once tried to dodge this by trying . . .
Not to.
Zacchaeus just taxed him for dying.
Everyone knew that this monstrous rate
Of taxation was far more than charged by the
state.
The truth was that when taxes started to rocket,

85

The money went straight in Zacchaeus's pocket.
Zacchaeus!
When the factory workers were paid, he was
    there,
Relieving them all of his usual share.
The chef hadn't much when Zacchaeus had
    finished,
His pay packet almost entirely diminished.
And down on the farm at the end of the day,
When the workers were paid in their usual way,
With a glint in his eye and a bulging great sack
To collect all his ill-gotten gains, waited Zacc.
Zacchaeus!
On Saturday morning the town was humming.
Everybody knew – someone special was coming.
He couldn't stay long – he was just passing
    through,
People got up early just to get a good view.
Everyone in Jericho was out on the street.
The crowds were pressing forward; they all
    wanted to meet
The teacher, the preacher, who healed with his
    hands,
The so-compelling, glory-telling miracle man!
Jesus!
Out on the streets, the excitement was mounting,
Inside Zacchaeus was deep in accounting:

| | |
|---|---|
| ZACC | Six and five is eleven – that's right – carry two . . . |
| CROWD | Will you get off my foot? Ow! Now look at my shoe! |
| ZACC | Forty and two's forty-two – is that all? |
| CROWD | Look, why can't you stand at the back? You're too tall! |

ZACC    Which makes my grand total five hundred and three . . .

CROWD   Mum!
        What is it now?
        Mummy, I need a –
        With a cry of frustration, Zacc slammed shut his book,
        And rushed from the house with a furious look.
        What could be worth the excitement and yelling?
        Who was expected? And what were they selling?
        He asked someone. 'Selling?' She said, 'don't be funny.
        Or have you forgotten, *you've* got all our money!'
        He pressed and he pushed as he tried to get through
        To the front of the crowd, so he'd get a good view,
        Past farmers and waiters, with their wives, children, aunts,
        He fought through the crowd in the hope of a glance
        Of this miracle worker whose fame and renown
        Had reached every village, every city and town,
        He even tried shouting 'Stand clear, he won't see us!'
        The people replied, 'He won't want to, Zacchaeus!
        This man is everything good, kind and true.
        Do you think that he'll want to meet someone like you?'
        Zacchaeus!
        Just then, the crowd surged. From far off came a cheer,

And a ripple of voices: 'He's here! Look! He's
    here!'
Zacchaeus was desperate. He just couldn't see.
What could he do? Then he saw it – a tree.
The cheering got louder – he had just enough
    time,
He tore off his sandals and started to climb.
The people all laughed as he shinned up the
    trunk:
'Look! He thinks he's a squirrel!' 'More like a
    skunk!'
Zacc climbed up and up, clutching branch, twig
    and leaf,
Until finally he stopped, looked and called with
    relief:

ZACC    'I may look absurd perched in this sapling,
But I'm one up on you – *I* can see what is
    happening!'
No one called back. A hush fell on the crowd.
And out of the silence, Zacc heard, clear and
    loud:

JESUS    'Zacchaeus – yes, you – can you hear me up there?
The one with no sandals, and leaves in your hair,
You don't look too comfortable up in that tree.
Shall we go to your house? I could do with some
    tea.'
Zacchaeus???
For Zacchaeus the weekend had been quite
    eventful,
But people returning to work were resentful.
'It just isn't fair,' they all started to mutter,
'That Zacchaeus, whose morals belong in the
    gutter,

That he – of all people – had Jesus to dinner.
A villain! A scoundrel! An outcast! A sinner!'
Tempers were rising. Enough was enough!
A meeting was called. They agreed to get tough.
They talked and discussed it. This was the
    consensus:
'Let's creep up behind him, and then knock him
    senseless!'
But who should appear at this moment, but Zacc,
With a smile on his face and his bulging great
    sack.
Zacchaeus!

ZACC    'New taxes!' he said, 'But before you turn blue,
These ones are taxes that I pay to you!'
'That *he* pays to *us*?' The mob stopped in its
    tracks.
Could Zacc have invented the first tax on tax?

ZACC    'A fifty per cent tax because I've been greedy,
For the poor, and for beggars, and those who are
    needy.
And this is the big one – four hundred per cent
To all who have suffered because I've been bent!'
And with that he opened his huge money sack,
And in handfuls of cash started giving it back.
And to every person he'd cheated, he promised
From now on his dealings with them would be
    honest.
Madness? A miracle? How do you start
To explain such a total, complete change of
    heart?
Nobody's sure, but on this they agree:
Zacc's changed since the day he had Jesus to tea.

# Girls' Talk (1)
## by Bridget Foreman

ANGE *13, struggling with the onset of puberty*
SAM *13, her friend, also struggling*

In many situations this sketch and its companion piece *Girls'
Talk (2),* which follows below, are useful discussion starters.
Within a longer sequence of sketches, if both pieces are used, the
return of characters which the audience has already begun to get
to know is a strength and also, of course, suggests the possibil-
ity that SAM and ANGE could be discovered discussing a whole
range of other subjects as well. But that's for another book or
your own creativity.

# Girls' Talk (1)

*Sam and Ange are in the school loos, examining their faces in the mirror, facing the audience. Ange is having a really good squeeze at a spot which is developing on her chin.*

ANGE      Ow!

SAM      Well, leave it alone, then!

ANGE      I can't. It's one of those volcanic under-the-surface ones. If I don't get rid of it now it'll erupt, probably at some crucially tender moment with Terry.

SAM      (*With the air of someone about to make an incredible revelation*) Speaking of crucially tender moments . . . take a squinny at this.

      (*She produces a pendant on a chain round her neck*)

ANGE      What's that?

SAM      My Simon gave it to me. It's a lover's heart.

ANGE      Couldn't he afford a whole one?

SAM      You're such a wazzock sometimes. It's *s'posed* to be like that. It's a symbol of our eternal union.

ANGE      Eternal? You only met him on Tuesday night.

SAM      Are you listening?

ANGE      Yes, go on. Eternal.

SAM      Y'see, he keeps one half, and he gives me the other. (*With great pretension*) Only together are they complete.

ANGE      Oh, that's dead meaningful, that is.

SAM      (*Dreamily*) Mm . . . meaningful . . .

ANGE      So it's a bit like those AIDS ribbons?

SAM      Y'what?

| | |
|---|---|
| ANGE | Those ribbons people wear for that AIDS charity. It's s'posed to show that they identify with AIDS sufferers. It shows what they care about. |
| SAM | Yeah, I s'pose it's a bit like that. |
| ANGE | Or like wearing a wedding ring, to show your commitment to another person? |
| SAM | There's no need to get too carried away. It's only a chain. Anyway, what've *you* got round *your* neck? |
| ANGE | (*Produces a chain*) |
| | Oh, that funny old cross thingy. What does that mean? |
| ANGE | Don't know. Nothing, I expect. |
| SAM | So why d'you wear it? |
| ANGE | My nan gave it to me for my christening. |
| SAM | Oh, yeah. Mine gave me one too, only mine's got a little man on. |
| ANGE | Ooh, I like those better. Do you want to do a swap? |
| SAM | Won't your nan notice? |
| ANGE | Shouldn't think so: she's blind. (*As they leave*) Actually, she's not very well at the moment . . . |

# Girls' Talk (2)
## by Bridget Foreman

SAM *13, struggling with metaphysical concepts*
ANGE *13, her friend, also struggling with big questions of life . . . and death*

# Girls' Talk (2)

*Two young teenage girls are waiting outside after school.*

SAM      Isn't your mum pickin' you up tonight, then?

ANGE      No, she can't. She's gone to the seaside with me nan.

SAM      (*Gently*) Ange, your nan died two weeks ago.

ANGE      I know that, birdbrain.

SAM      Then how has your mum gone to the seaside with her?

ANGE      Ashes.

SAM      What?

ANGE      With her ashes. Mum's gone to the seaside with my nan's ashes. Nan had this thing about Blackpool. She met Grandad on the pier there, and she said she wanted her ashes to be scattered from Blackpool Tower.

SAM      Oh, yuck! I hope there's no one on the beach doing their sun-tan lotion at the same time. So she was cremulated, then?

ANGE      *Cremated.*

SAM      Yeah, that's what I said. (*Pause*) What was it like?

ANGE      Dunno – a bit, well . . . remote, really. We all went into this room. There was music playing –

SAM      Music?

ANGE      Yeah, sort of plastic music. A bit like the stuff they play in the lift at the motel, only more depressing.

SAM      Oh, my God. Then what?

ANGE      Then this vicar bloke read out some stuff about

heaven and that, in a voice like a wet weekend. It didn't sound much fun. And then there was a sort of whirring sound, and nan's coffin disappeared behind a pair of spangly curtains. That was it.

SAM   (*Troubled*) And do you think that *is* it?

ANGE   What do you mean?

SAM   Well, is that all there is? I mean, do we go through all this just to disappear through a pair of spangly curtains and end up stuck in the sun-tan lotion on someone's bum? What about all that stuff about heaven?

ANGE   That's just words. They say all that to make you feel better about dying. I can't see my nan sitting on a cloud with a harp. They'd never get the TV remote out of her hand, just for a start.

SAM   But leaving out the angels in frilly nighties, don't you sometimes think there must be something else – somewhere else?

(*Ange goes all 'spooky' and sings the theme to* The Twilight Zone)

SAM   Oh, come on! I'm serious, Ange. Doesn't it worry you?

ANGE   I s'pose the funeral did make me think a bit. But it's just fairy stories. I mean, there's no proof about heaven, is there?

SAM   So where's your nan now, then?

ANGE   I don't know. Nowhere. I think she's just – dead. (*Pause*) Oh, will you look at us? Anyone would think we were dead, an' all! (*They start to leave*) Hey, there's a party round Alison's tonight. Are you coming?

SAM   Don't know yet. Can I come round yours to get ready?

# Personal Columns
## by Nigel Forde

ONE *a young woman expecting her first baby*
TWO *a woman about to get married*
THREE *a man wishing he could stop thinking about death*

This sketch is stylised along the lines of a familiar comic format. However, the key to a successful performance is for each actor to discover (and to deliver) a precise, living reality within each moment and behind each line. That can be achieved in a hundred slightly varying ways: by focusing on the thoughts which give each line motivation; perhaps speaking in response to another person whom we never see; varying the intonation and level of their voice; imagining that some lines are spoken to someone listening from another room; and so on and so on. If the actors can produce three-dimensional characters, fully alive within their own worlds, the stylised framework of the sketch will then serve to help the audience understand the point and be looking out for the punchline. It is therefore important that the three actors don't develop a way of saying their lines (within each triplet) that implies they have just been listening to the previous speaker.

# Personal Columns

*Very little movement is useful in this piece, though it may be helpful to stage it with the actors standing/sitting at different levels and to place the man between the two women so he becomes the central focus. The actors should try and avoid being in one straight line facing the audience. They speak in their own little worlds.*

| | |
|---|---|
| ONE | Birth. |
| TWO | Marriage. |
| THREE | Death. |

| | |
|---|---|
| ONE | I can't believe it's really going to happen. |
| TWO | I can't believe it's really going to happen. |
| THREE | I can't believe it's really going to happen. |

| | |
|---|---|
| ONE | I must admit, I'm a bit nervous. |
| TWO | I must say, I do get a few butterflies from time to time. |
| THREE | I am utterly and desperately terrified. |

| | |
|---|---|
| ONE | I feel whole, fulfilled! |
| TWO | I feel wonderful, radiant! |
| THREE | I'm fine! Fine! . . . Honest! |

| | |
|---|---|
| ONE | I just can't wait for the moment. |
| TWO | I'm ticking off the days on the calendar. |
| THREE | Look, we'll cross that bridge when we come to it, eh? |

| | |
|---|---|
| ONE | I've done up the nursery, booked the ante-natal classes and bought a lovely buggy. |
| TWO | I've chosen the dress, booked St Bart's for the twentieth and been through the menu with the caterer. |
| THREE | Yeah, well, I've been a bit pushed recently, so, er . . . |
| | |
| ONE | I'm doing all the exercises, watching my diet, reading the books. |
| TWO | I've ordered the cake, I've chosen the flowers, and we're going to marriage preparation classes. |
| THREE | Well . . . what can I do? |
| | |
| ONE | My mum's been ever so helpful. |
| TWO | My mother-in-law's been a tower of strength. |
| THREE | I'm on my own, aren't I? |
| | |
| ONE | She says I'm wide-eyed with wonder. |
| TWO | She's helped us go into this with our eyes wide open. |
| THREE | I'll just shut my eyes and hope for the best. |
| | |
| ONE | I don't want to know what sex my baby is. |
| TWO | I don't want to know where we're going for the honeymoon. |
| THREE | I don't want to know, all right? |
| | |
| ONE | I'm so excited, I can't stop talking about it! |
| TWO | I talk about nothing else, all the time! |
| THREE | Look, let's talk about something else, shall we? |
| | |
| ONE | I think I'm ready: I've done everything I can. |

| | |
|---|---|
| TWO | I'm all prepared: there's nothing more I can do. |
| THREE | I've done nothing. |
| | |
| ONE | Midwives, gynaecologists, doctors – they're all experienced. They all know what's what. |
| TWO | Bridesmaids, organist, choir – we've had a rehearsal and it'll all be fine. |
| THREE | I just wish there was someone who could tell you what to expect. |
| | |
| ONE | Of course, a new baby is just the beginning. |
| TWO | Of course, the wedding itself is just the start. |
| THREE | Death is . . . I mean, death . . . Death is only . . . |
| | |
| ONE | It's afterwards everything's going to be different. |
| TWO | It's afterwards that the big change comes. |
| THREE | It's afterwards . . . |
| | |
| ONE | I keep telling myself it's going to happen! |
| TWO | It's really, really going to happen! |
| | (*Pause*) |
| THREE | Nah! |

# Into His Courts
## by Nigel Forde

EMMA *a barrister*
CHARLES WESTERHAM *a barrister, her colleague*
DARRYL NUGENT *a man seeking to bring his case to court. A bit of a wide-boy but extremely thick with it.*

# Into His Courts

*A barrister's office. Emma is sorting through some papers. After a moment, Charles enters briskly, ready to start a new day.*

CHARLES      Emma! Lovely to see you back. Good holiday? What have we got to enthrall us this morning?

EMMA      (*Guardedly*) Um . . . it's in the book.

CHARLES      (*Glances through the appointment book*)

CHARLES      Nugent versus . . . (*Difficult to read*) Rod? Is it? Or Gold? Ten fifteen. Well (*Glances at watch*), any minute now, then.

EMMA      (*Quietly but distinctly*) God!

CHARLES      What is it, Emma? Are you all right?

EMMA      Fine. I just said 'God'.

CHARLES      Yes, I know.

EMMA      That's the word you couldn't read. Nugent versus 'God'.
(*There is a slight pause, then Charles chuckles*)
What's the matter?

CHARLES      Nothing. It's just that I thought you said our ten fifteen was Nugent versus *God!*
(*Charles chuckles again*)

EMMA      I did. Darryl Geoffrey Hurst Livingstone Nugent apparently woke one morning and looked round at a world from which all traces of God's goodness seemed to have disappeared. God had not exalted the humble and meek, and the rich he had definitely failed to send empty away. This, to Mr Nugent, seemed unfair. He decided to sue God.

CHARLES      To sue God! Why, for heaven's sake?

EMMA            Breach of promise, discrimination, loss of earn-
                ings, unfair treatment, you name it.
                (*There is a knock at the door*)
EMMA            That will probably be him now.
                (*She opens the door and Nugent comes in. Slightly
                out of his depth and suspicious, but assuming an air
                of confidence*)
CHARLES         Ah, Mr Nugent.
NUGENT          (*Narrows his eyes*) Who wants to know?
EMMA            This is Charles Westerham, Mr Nugent. If we
                take your case, he'll be representing you.
NUGENT          Fair enough. All right, Charlie?
CHARLES         Er, sit down Mr Nugent. Now, you'll admit this
                case poses us something of a problem.
NUGENT          Oh yeah?
CHARLES         Not the least of which is – and correct me if I'm
                wrong – that you wish to bring into court the God
                of Abraham and Isaac, the Ancient of Days.
NUGENT          Come again?
EMMA            Jahweh. The Lord God Almighty, creator of all
                things visible and invisible, the triune deity, con-
                substantial, co-eternal, the ineffable and everlast-
                ing Father.
NUGENT          Yeah, that's the one.
CHARLES         May I ask why?
NUGENT          Lossa reasons, really. But mainly on account of
                him being pavilioned in splendour and girded
                with praise whereas yours truly has got naff all.
CHARLES         Kings do tend to be more rich and powerful than
                their subjects.
EMMA            And this particular King is, after all, *creator coeli
                et terrae.*
NUGENT          Say again?

| | |
|---|---|
| CHARLES | Maker of heaven and earth – *creator coeli et terrae.* |
| NUGENT | Yeah. Right. That's fine. He can be . . . grey Arthur of jelly and terror. I jus' want a bit more of the jelly and a bit less of the terror. I'm only askin' for what I'm entitled to. |
| CHARLES | Really? |
| NUGENT | Stands to reason. |
| EMMA | I'm sure you think it does. |
| NUGENT | OK. God has created us, right? And he loves us, every single one of us, wiv a deep an' sacrificial love from everlastin' to – wossname? – everlastin'. So that includes me. God loves me, deeply an' wivaht reserve. |
| | (*There is quite a long silence*) |
| | Well then, I want to be showered wiv blessings. I mean, he *says* he loves me, but I don't see much practical evidence of it, know what I mean? I want a life of romance and glamour and riches. I want a yacht and a car and a race horse. I want a Tudor farmhouse in Devon and a hillside villa in Cannes. I want breakfast with Zoë Ball, lunch with Kate Winslet and supper with Denise Van Outen, and (*takes out small catalogue*) I'd really like a pair of these stone-washed jeans. |
| EMMA | (*Playing along*) The grey or the blue? |
| NUGENT | The grey, I think. |
| EMMA | Yes. They'd suit you. |
| CHARLES | No, no, no. I'm sorry. The whole thing is a ridiculous fantasy. |
| EMMA | He's right, I'm afraid. No one wears stonewashed jeans any more. |
| CHARLES | What makes you think you deserve all this special treatment? |

| | |
|---|---|
| NUGENT | Other people are happy, glamorous, loaded with money. Haven't you read your Palms? |
| CHARLES | Good gracious, no! |
| NUGENT | Well, you should. |
| CHARLES | Occult practices, I'm afraid, are rather frowned on . . . |
| NUGENT | No, the Book of Palms. The Palms of David. |
| CHARLES | Ah, I see. |
| NUGENT | (*Quoting*) 'Lo, these are the wicked. These prosper in the world, and these have riches in possession.' |
| EMMA | Quite. But . . . |
| NUGENT | 'All they that see me laugh me to scorn. They shoot out their lips. "Tush," they say.' |
| CHARLES | Do they? |
| NUGENT | Yes, they flamin' do, and I've had enough of it. I'm a laughing stock. |
| EMMA | So you think it's God's duty to provide you with lorryfulls of material goods to make you feel better about your life? |
| NUGENT | That's about the size of it. |
| CHARLES | And where did you get that idea from – Paul's Epistle to *The Simpsons*? |
| NUGENT | Sorry? |
| CHARLES | Nothing, nothing. |
| EMMA | There is also the technical problem of actually getting God to appear in the courtroom. I'm not sure of the procedures for sub-poenaing the Almighty. |
| NUGENT | No probs. Charlie here is representing me – God can send someone to represent him. |
| CHARLES | But what if everybody started suing God because things weren't working out the way they wanted? |

|          | It would be chaos. You think that God owes you a happy and blessed life? |
|----------|--------------------------------------------------------------------------|
| NUGENT   | Yup. |
| CHARLES  | A life of material comfort and personal pleasure. |
| NUGENT   | 'Sright. A land flowing with milk and money. |
| EMMA     | Honey. |
| NUGENT   | Scholars are divided on the correct translation. |
| CHARLES  | But why just you? |
| NUGENT   | No, no – not just me. Everybody's entitled to it. |
| CHARLES  | Everybody? Including me? |
| NUGENT   | Werl, I s'pose so, yeah. |
| CHARLES  | All right. Then suppose that I could only find fulfilment and true happiness by punching you in the mouth and kicking you down the stairs. Should God let me do that? |
| NUGENT   | That's different. |
| CHARLES  | Is it? Suppose your nextdoor neighbour found genuine pleasure in flower arrangement and took all your flowers in order to indulge his pleasure. |
| EMMA     | Suppose Zoë Ball's husband would rather you didn't have breakfast with her? |
| CHARLES  | Suppose the race horse, the yacht and the Tudor farmhouse weren't for sale. How could you be entitled to them? |
| NUGENT   | You're just confusing me. |
| EMMA     | They're the sort of questions the defence would be bound to raise. |
| NUGENT   | (*With a knowing wag of his finger*) If he thought of them. |
| CHARLES  | But God is omniscient . . . which puts us at something of a disadvantage in the matter of surprise. |
| EMMA     | I think you have to accept, Mr Nugent, that there is no right to happiness, because if everybody |

claimed it, nobody, paradoxically, could be happy.

NUGENT    (*After a pause*) Sorry, that's too deep for me.

CHARLES   Mr. Nugent, even the kiddies' paddling pool at Clacton Waterworld is too deep for you.

NUGENT    Eh?

CHARLES   Maybe God has something better for you than all the things you *think* you want.

NUGENT    I *know* I want them!

EMMA      Would you like a Noddy book to read?

NUGENT    Eh?

EMMA      A cuddly toy to take your mind off things? A plate of fish fingers?

NUGENT    Do me a favour!

CHARLES   But you wanted those things when you were three, didn't you?

NUGENT    Come off it! I've changed since I was three!

EMMA      Maybe you will again.

NUGENT    (*Suspicious of that last remark*) You what?

CHARLES   I think Emma is saying that what we think is important or good or necessary one day, we may not want at all another day.

EMMA      We change. Maybe the closer we get to God the more we'll find a match between what we want and what he gives us.

          (*Nugent and Charles give her a quizzical look*)

          Well, it stands to reason. It's logic. You can't invent a character for God and then blame him for what you've invented. It's plain stupid.

CHARLES   So I should settle out of court, Mr Nugent.

NUGENT    And how do I do that?

CHARLES   You seem well acquainted with the Book of . . . Palms. 'Lift up your voice in supplication' . . .

EMMA          'Wait patiently upon the Lord.'

NUGENT        Werl . . . I dunno. Why should he listen to me?

CHARLES       Personally, I can't see any reason.

EMMA          Only, the odd thing is, he said he would. It's worth
              a try.

NUGENT        (*Thinks for a moment, then stands decisively*) All
              right, but if it doesn't work I'll be back.
              (*He goes*)

# Sex! Wassitallabout?
## by Antony Dunn

A GROUP OF ACTORS *both boys and girls; a minimum of two of each*

Like other similar sketches in this collection, the text here is the first building block in the creation of your own piece of physical theatre, involving rhythm, mime and lightning cameo characters in familiar situations. Each line or verse will suggest a context for you to visualise with stylised, economic movement; then you can make appropriate decisions about whether the lines are spoken by 'the boys' or 'the girls' or by couples or individuals. The allocations made in the margin are obviously not the only possibilities. The rhythm of the piece is based on the general rule of four beats to each line. After verse one there is a suggested *'Ooh! Aah! Ooh-ooh, ah!'* which might be used throughout both as an underscore or as a 'fill' between verses. It is meant to be delivered with that same quality of self-conscious seriousness and lustful desire that we get on endless perfume and aftershave commercials.

# Sex! Wassitallabout?

*The rhythm builds up stealthily as the sketch begins. First one voice emerges, then two, three, then everyone together on the fourth line.*

It's on the television, it's on the radio,
it's in every magazine, it's at the movie show,
it's on the internet, the megadrive and video,
it's coming in by satellite (*one voice, slowing*) to
   everywhere I go.
*Ooh ah, ooh ooh ah*
*ooh ah, ooh ooh ah . . .*

BOYS After school, me and Rick
behind the bikesheds with a year-ten chick;
now that's what I call education,
biology for our generation.

GIRLS It says in my magazine – so it's true –
'It' can make a woman of you,
classy, beautiful and chic.
Oh shut up, mum, I'm sixteen next week.

BOYS Friday night, chasing skirt –
babe, score, pull, oi darlin', flirt!
Out with the boys, gotta do the stuff.
What's the matter, Rick, not man enough?

GIRLS Saturday night we're in together,
Rick says he can't wait for ever.
*Come on – let's do it, before it's too late.*

I wonder if I should maybe wait?
(*Rhythm stops abruptly*)

COUPLE     NAAAH! *(Rhythm starts again)*

GIRLS      We're great together, we're a perfect match,
           and when you itch you've got to scratch.
           Don't save it for some far-off day!
           *Feels like I've given a piece of myself away* . . .

BOYS       Don't get tied down and don't waste time,
           get your kicks while you're in your prime;
           and most of all, avoid like rabies
           any girl who mentions (*mime 'babies'*).

GIRLS      Down in accounts there's a bloke called Jim
           who says he'd like me to sleep with him.
           Now I'm not as young as I used to be
           and it's nice that someone still fancies me . . .

           If there's something missing, if you feel the lack,
           just think of England as you lie back.
           At the end of the day, when push comes to shove
           never, ever mention lo . . .
           (*Rhythm stops*)

BOYS       Roses are red and bruises are blue,
           and it hurts me more than it hurts you.
           Notches on bed-heads and adding up exes
           are the scores on the doors in the battle of sexes.

GIRLS      Four am by the telephone –
           I didn't choose to sleep alone,

the stains on sheets, the empty bed,
the clinic, the panic, the wishing I was dead . . .

Middle-aged, single mum,
down the social, here we come.
Button it! Just push the carriage,
and never, ever mention ma . . .

(*Voices drop out one by one, SFX tuning radio*)
I saw it on the television, heard it on the radio,
saw it in a magazine, saw it at the movie show,
found it on the internet, the megadrive and video,
and yes, I could have waited, but I couldn't say
   no.

# Roses
## by David Brooks

ONE *a man in search of flowers*
TWO *a florist*

Every now and then a sketch comes along which genuinely works like one of Jesus' parables – you suspect that you know what it means, but it is simply a story which works in its own right and you have to go away and chew it over to discover within it the values of the kingdom of God. This is one of those. At face value it is a brief episode in the life of a man who cannot understand how anything in the modern world can be free and cannot change his pattern of behaviour to carry away the freebie which is offered to him . . . even when it is clearly to his advantage. Because the 'meaning' of this sketch could apply to several aspects of the Christian gospel, Roughshod has found it to be a useful sketch – often placed at the end of a sequence of sketches, almost as an afterthought. A good performance needs good pace and good timing between the two actors.

# Roses

*A man carrying many bulging refuse bags rushes into a florist's just on closing time.*

| | |
|---|---|
| ONE | Oh! Thank goodness you're open! I wanted to buy a flower for my sweetheart. |
| TWO | Well, we only have rose bushes, and they're free. |
| ONE | I was actually looking for some chrysanthemums. |
| TWO | I'm sorry, we only have rose bushes. |
| ONE | No dahlias? |
| TWO | No. |
| ONE | Poms? |
| TWO | No. |
| ONE | Daffodils? |
| TWO | No. |
| ONE | Delphiniums? |
| TWO | No. |
| ONE | Potentilla atrosanguinea? |
| TWO | No. |
| ONE | Achilea filipendulina? |
| TWO | I'm sorry, we only have rose bushes. |
| ONE | No tulips, then? |
| TWO | No. |
| ONE | Only roses? |
| TWO | Yes. Only rose bushes. |
| ONE | Do you think roses would be romantic? |
| TWO | Yes, very romantic. |
| ONE | I'll have a rose, then. |
| | (*The florist hands him a bush of red roses in a pot*) |
| ONE | No no – I just want the one rose. |

| | |
|---|---|
| TWO | But you can have the whole bush. |
| ONE | No, I just need the one. I'll just take the one. A whole bush would be a bit overpowering. I was going to say to her, 'A perfect rose for my perfect rose.' 'A perfect rose bush for my perfect rose bush' doesn't sound quite right. And anyway, I couldn't afford a whole bush. |
| TWO | But it's free. And if you took the whole bush, you'd have an endless supply of perfect roses for your perfect rose. |
| ONE | I suppose I could give you a cheque. |
| TWO | I don't want your cheques. |
| ONE | (*Hurt*) I have a cheque guarantee card! |
| TWO | I don't want payment. It's free! Take it! (*Pause*) |
| ONE | Do you take Visa? |
| TWO | No. |
| ONE | Mastercard? |
| TWO | No. |
| ONE | American Express? |
| TWO | No. |
| ONE | Won't that do nicely? |
| TWO | No, it won't! Listen – it's free. F – R – E – E, FREE! |
| ONE | Free? |
| TWO | Yes. |
| ONE | No charge? |
| TWO | No. |
| ONE | Nothing at all? |
| TWO | No. |
| ONE | I see. |
| TWO | Good. (*Pause*) |

| | |
|---|---|
| ONE | Will you take an IOU, then? |
| TWO | Aarrgh! Listen! This rose bush is yours for the princely sum of nothing. Or, in monetary terms, zero pounds, zero pence and zero per cent VAT. All you have to do is pick it up and take it away. You owe me nothing. Do you understand? |
| ONE | Yes. |
| TWO | Phew. |
| ONE | I'll take one. So when's your earliest delivery date? |
| TWO | Just take this one now. |
| ONE | Oh, I can't do that. |
| TWO | Why not? |
| ONE | Well, I've got my hands full with these bags, you see. |
| TWO | What's in your bags? |
| ONE | Oh, nothing much. Rubbish, mainly. Well, in fact it's all rubbish, now I think about it. Can't seem to get rid of it. No one seems to want it. |
| TWO | Just leave your rubbish here, then, and take your rose bush. I'll deal with your rubbish. |
| ONE | Mind you, there's some good quality rubbish in here. Look at this piece of newspaper – had some good quality fish wrapped in that. |
| TWO | Doesn't matter what it is – just leave your rubbish here and take your rose bush. |
| ONE | And when do I come back for my rubbish? |
| TWO | Never. I'll deal with that. |
| ONE | You'll get rid of all my rubbish? |
| TWO | Yes. |
| ONE | Hmm . . . |

(*He carefully puts down his bags and takes the rose bush while trying to work the deal out in his head*)

So what you're saying is that, if I want, I can leave

|       | all my rubbish here, and take away this rose bush – free of charge – and it's mine to keep for ever, at no extra cost? |
|-------|------|
| TWO   | Precisely! |
| ONE   | Right. |
| TWO   | So you'll take it? |
|       | (*Pause*) |
| ONE   | I'll think about it. |
|       | (*He quickly replaces the bush on the counter, picks up his bags and hurries out of the shop*) |

# The Heavenly City
## by Paul Burbridge

A GROUP OF ACTORS *working as an ensemble, physically and vocally. The text here indicates four actors but the exact size of the group can be determined by the director*

The first version of this piece was performed solo by the mime artist Geoffrey Stevenson and the words were part of a soundtrack with music by Chris Norton. That is worth mentioning if only to encourage those who might wish to take a similar approach with the current version printed here. The subject has a breadth and a dignity which may also make it a contender for performance in a context which requires a certain sobriety, even at a funeral, since it focuses on the faith that looks beyond death to the glory of heaven.

# The Heavenly City

*The first section reminds us of all the richness and the detail of life which is available to us through our senses – all in fact that death appears to take away from us. The actors illustrate the words with actions. This opening mime sequence should establish a vigorous, tangible world of people, objects and experiences explored through the five senses. It is a world of relationships, eating and drinking, building, activity, exploring nature, getting wet, cooking, wind, solid objects, laughter, tears, death, gravestones, rock, flowers, birth, writing, books, games . . . etc.*

*In sequence they take one word each and accompany it with an action.*

> Eyes – colour, search, distance, change
> Hands – clutch, smooth, climb, put together
> Nose – breathe, perfume, discover, warning
> Mouth – bite, bitter, speak, kiss
> Ears – shout, attentive, whisper, respond
> Death – this little world, an ending.
> (*Recapitulating five of the previous images*)
> Shape, texture, smell, language, sound
> Yet death. This little world, an ending.
> (*They continue to illustrate the text with strong physical pictures*)

| | |
|---|---|
| ONE | Faith, |
| TWO | a window. |
| THREE | Death, |
| FOUR | a door. |
| ONE | Beyond, |
| TWO | an invisible strength, |

129

| | |
|---|---|
| FOUR | the word of God, |
| THREE | a better country, |
| FOUR | not yet. |
| TWO | From the beginning, faith has been a window. |
| ONE | Abel offered worship, |
| | God called him righteous, |
| | He was brutally murdered. |
| | His faith still speaks. |
| TWO | Enoch pleased God so much |
| | God took him away. |
| | His leaving was instant. |
| | His faith has no grave. |
| THREE | Noah heeded God's warning, |
| | Became heir to righteousness. |
| | His household was saved. |
| | His faith brings a rainbow. |
| FOUR | Abraham answered God's call |
| | In pursuit of a promise. |
| | Homeless and old, |
| | His faith was rewarded. |
| ONE | Sarah believed God against nature. |
| | He gave her a child |
| | Whose life was protected. |
| | Her faith brought new life. |
| TWO | Moses fought for God's justice. |
| | He upheld the poor, |
| | Delivered from death. |
| | His faith freed a nation. |
| THREE | Mary offered up herself. |
| | God, born his daughter's son. |
| | His death pierced her soul. |
| | Her faith brought a saviour. |
| FOUR | These all died in faith, |

| | |
|---|---|
| TWO | staring through the open window. |
| ONE | They saw what was to come. |
| THREE | Faith is no escape from now. It blazes in the teeth of torture, chains, violence, affliction, |
| FOUR | It burns brightest under poverty, mockery, home-lessness, abuse, decay. |
| ONE | It is strength out of weakness, |
| TWO | Greater wealth |
| FOUR | Than all the treasures |
| THREE | Of Egypt. The reward is not yet. |
| TWO | We see it through the window of faith. |
| THREE | We enter through the door, |
| FOUR | Face to face with hope. |
| ONE | Those who die in faith, do not die. |
| FOUR | They wait to receive the promise. |
| TWO | God has prepared for them a city. |
| FOUR | Whoever would draw near to God must believe God rewards those who seek him. |
| THREE | Life – |
| TWO | This invisible world, a beginning. |
| ONE | For he has built them a city. |

(*The group freeze*)

## Barabbas – The Substitute
### by Bridget Foreman

BARABBAS *a criminal, reprieved by Pontius Pilate*
SIMON *his friend*

# Barabbas – The Substitute

*It is Easter Eve. Barabbas has been up all night following Friday's crucifixions. He enters alone, bottle in hand.*

BARABBAS    'Go on,' he says – 'clear off, before the Governor changes his mind.' And I'm supposed to be grateful. It's hot. And everyone's heading up to the hill. So I go too – never one to miss a good show, me. There's three of 'em – a couple of likely lookers – didn't know 'em, but I could have done. Scallys – not too bright – got caught. Course, they're shouting and screaming, all the usual stuff. One of them's only young – about the age I was when I got started. Then there's this other one – all quiet. There's people chucking stuff, shouting . . . and it's almost like he's somewhere else. I mean, he's there all right – you could see it, *really* see it in him – every muscle, every sinew, blood running down his face. But it was like he couldn't hear them, or see them. So I start – 'Wake up you stupid beggar!' and I start spitting. 'Course, it doesn't get anywhere near him – it hits the cross, dribbles down. And that's when I realise – it was mine, wasn't it?
(*Pause*)
I couldn't spit at him any more. Just stood and watched, for hours. It got darker and darker. He was mumbling stuff, calling out to God. Flies crawling all over his face, like he was already dead. How do you know? In all that, how do you

135

know when you're going? When can you can say, 'That's it. It's finished!'? How do you know it's not going to go on and on? (*He becomes more incoherent*) I mean, how much can you take? When's it going to end?

(*Enter Simon*)

SIMON   Come on, it's over. Barabbas!

(*Barabbas looks at him questioningly*)

Let's go, eh? Celebrate your release – toast the Romans! Come on.

BARABBAS   (*Blankly*) Yeah. Yeah, I'm coming.

# The Road to Emmaus
## by Paul Burbridge and Bridget Foreman

CLEOPAS *a disciple of Jesus, sensible, deeply middle-aged and wears motoring gloves*
ANNA *his wife, charming and emotional*
JESUS *a hitch-hiker, recently raised from the dead*

The background to this wonderful comic incident from the Gospel of Luke is discussed in more detail in the Introduction to this book. The fact that Jesus spent so long with these two people, about whom we know almost nothing, and that he cared so much for their state of heart and mind, that he enjoyed their company and spent so long expounding the Scriptures to them is of the utmost significance and encouragement to similar 'unknown' disciples like us. It's such a glowing example of how much each of us is loved by God, who is clearly no respecter of persons. Why did Jesus not appear to Pilate or to Herod or Caiaphas? Surely so much more would have been gained for the kingdom of God? The sense of power, of victory, would have been so much greater. It would have been perfect publicity. Yet Jesus chose to publicise his cosmic victory over sin and death among ordinary people – his friends, his disciples, those with whom he had spent his life. These were the people he could trust to be the living foundation stones of the

Christian church, with all their idiosyncrasies and familiar human foibles.

A concession to the modern era is that the walk back to Emmaus from Jerusalem has, in this sketch, become a journey in Cleopas' Ford Mondeo, in which Jesus will attempt to hitch a lift.

# The Road to Emmaus

*Cleopas and Anna are travelling towards the audience in a 'car'. Jesus is waiting at one side, holding a sign saying 'Emmaus'. Anna is overcome with grief. She is working her way through her third box of tissues. Cleopas attempts to get her to see the brighter side of things with relentless, if heavy-handed bonhomie from behind the wheel.*

CLEOPAS    Well, at least it was a decent send-off. All those vol-au-vents seemed to be very popular.

ANNA    (*Snivelling*) It doesn't make it any easier, though – now he's gone. I feel so empty.
(*She dissolves into tears*)

CLEOPAS    Obviously, I'm not suggesting that vol-au-vents make the death of Jesus any easier to cope with. I'm simply saying that the standard of catering can be a mark of respect at a funeral.
(*Stops the car with a sudden jerk to let an old person cross the road*)
Come on, you silly old fool! You can go across now!

ANNA    A cross!
(*More floods of tears*)

CLEOPAS    Oh, cheer up, love. What have I said? It comes to us all. He was only human.
(*The car moves off again*)

ANNA    He was supposed to be the Messiah.

CLEOPAS    Yes, until three o'clock on Friday afternoon.
(*Sees Jesus up ahead*)
Oh, look. Shall we give this poor lad a lift?

| | |
|---|---|
| ANNA | Not a hitch-hiker, Cleopas. You never know where they've been! |
| CLEOPAS | You know where they're going, though. He's got Emmaus on his sign. |
| | (*He brings the car to a tyre-squealing halt*) |
| ANNA | Just don't blame me if he's a psychopath. |
| CLEOPAS | Hop in mate! (*Under his breath*) As long as you're not a demented psychopath. |
| JESUS | Sorry? |
| CLEOPAS | Nothing. |
| JESUS | Cheers. |
| | (*Jesus climbs into the back seat, barely having time to shut the door before Cleopas gives the gear box some stick again*) |
| CLEOPAS | Where have you come from? My wife was interested to know. |
| JESUS | Jerusalem. |
| CLEOPAS | Terrible business, wasn't it? That execution. |
| ANNA | (*Beginning to blub again*) We've just come from the funeral. |
| JESUS | Was it someone close to you? |
| ANNA | Yes. |
| CLEOPAS | Not quite so close now, of course. |
| | (*Anna whimpers*) |
| | The wife's been feeling a little flat, poor love. (*Winking back at Jesus*) We're running out of tissues. |
| JESUS | Who was it? |
| CLEOPAS | Who was it? Who?! |
| JESUS | Yes, who? |
| CLEOPAS . | Dear, oh, dear! Don't you read the papers? What have you been doing in Jerusalem? Get a life, son! You must be the only person who doesn't know |

what's been going on there these last few days. A kind of prophet, called Jesus. Surely you've heard of him?

JESUS          Oh, yes. I've heard of him.

CLEOPAS        The High Priest, you see, thought he was getting too big for his sandals, so they executed him on some trumped-up charge of political subversion. (*The car swerves violently as Cleopas realises that he has not been giving full attention to the road ahead*)

               Whoopsie!

ANNA           We thought he was the Messiah come to rescue us.

CLEOPAS        Well, that was a bit wide of the mark, wasn't it?

ANNA           He was ever such a nice man. Healed my mother's leg last January. And now he's gone . . .
               (*More tears*)

CLEOPAS        Now, now, now.

JESUS          But he lives on, doesn't he?

CLEOPAS        'Course he does! On and on – in his words and in the memory of his actions. We've got some wonderful memories of all the things he did. And in a manner of speaking he's still with us. Right here in the car.

ANNA           But it's not the same. What use are memories?

CLEOPAS        Memories, my dear, are infinitely preferable to the sort of delusions that Mary is suffering from.

ANNA           (*To Jesus*) My friend Mary was very close to him.

CLEOPAS        About three feet away this morning, apparently.

ANNA           She thought she saw him this morning, doing the borders. Said she spoke to him and he was as real as you or I.

CLEOPAS        I think she gets flushes.

JESUS Maybe she did see him.

CLEOPAS (*Laughs*) He's as dead as a doornail. (*Anna whimpers about nails*) *Mat!* Sorry, door*mat!* Dear, oh, dear!

JESUS But he did say this would happen, didn't he? He said that the Messiah would have to die. But come back again after three days, risen from the dead.
(*As he says this, Jesus half-stands, stretching out his arms*)

CLEOPAS (*Catching sight of him doing this*) Oooh, do you want to stretch your legs, son? I tell you what – we'll stop for a cuppa. Do you fancy a cuppa? And a commemorative sandwich? They sent us away with a bag of left-overs.
(*The car lurches to another halt*)

ANNA In the tupperware in that basket beside you.

JESUS But it's not so strange, is it?

CLEOPAS No, they always make far too many sandwiches.

JESUS I meant Jesus keeping his word. That's not so strange. I mean, have you ever met Lazarus?

CLEOPAS What, that chap who came back from the dead? Now that was very unusual.

JESUS Living proof that Jesus had power over death, I'd say.

CLEOPAS Should we say grace?

ANNA A little prayer would be very nice, thank you, dear.
(*They bow their heads. Slight pause. Cleopas opens his mouth and draws breath to say grace, but Jesus suddenly cuts in*)

JESUS Father, thank you for your mighty power. Thank you for these friends and their food. And thank you that Mary was right.

(*Jesus disappears. Cleopas and Anna do a double-take*)

(*At this point they can either freeze to indicate the end of the sketch, or this narrative link can be used to continue into another sketch –* Wrapped Fish . . .)

(*Cleopas and Anna share the lines*)

CLEOPAS    Whammo! Gone! In the blink of an eye,

ANNA    But alive – the Jesus we saw die.

CLEOPAS    With a squeal of tyres and a gear-change crunch
They sped to Jerusalem in time for lunch.
They could hardly contain their excitement at giving
The news to the others – Jesus was living!

ANNA    They tore up the stairs at 'The Goat and Cheeses',
Burst through the door – and there he was . . . Jesus!
(*Cleopas and Anna clearly feel their news is somewhat redundant. They back out of the room sheepishly, smiling*)

CLEOPAS    Hello, Thomas!

ANNA    After a while everyone knew
That Jesus was living – the rumours were true.

CLEOPAS    There were parties, rejoicing, all over town,
But after a while, life settled down . . .
(*The action moves into the beginning of* Wrapped Fish)

# Wrapped Fish
## by Bridget Foreman

A GROUP OF ACTORS; *this can be larger than the four indicated below, between whom the text has been shared out.*

Another example of a story-telling sketch, set to a strong rhythm – in this case the chugging rhythm of a small fishing boat engine. All the actors take responsibility for keeping the rhythm going when they are not speaking and they all share in creating the picture of a weary crew who have spent a fruitless (or perhaps that should be fishless) night on the water. A perfectly believable 'boat' can be staged with, say, four chairs . . . the key as always is the attitude of the actors. If they believe in what they are doing and communicate that belief, then they will transport the audience to Galilee and back.

# Wrapped Fish

| | |
|---|---|
| PAUL | We were all out fishing one night |
| | But with no success |
| VICKI | Not a sprat in sight. |
| BRIDGET | The water was still, the bait was wriggling |
| | But as for the fish they just weren't nibbling. |
| MARK | We worked on and on with mounting frustration |
| | But couldn't pull in even one crustacean. |
| PAUL | At three in the morning, a final trawl |
| | Brought in half a wellie |
| | (*With Bridget*) and a flat beach ball. |
| | (*The rhythm subsides and they sink into a motionless silence. After a while*:) |
| | I spy with my little eye, something beginning with 'S'. |
| BRIDGET | (*Deeply bored*) Stars. |
| PAUL | Nope. |
| MARK | Sea. |
| PAUL | Yup. |
| VICKI | (*Pointing excitedly into the water*) |
| | I spy with my little eye, something beginning with 'F'!! |
| MARK | Fish! |
| VICKI | No. (*Waving it at him irritatingly*) Finger. |
| PAUL | (*Suddenly seeing something*) I spy with my little eye, something beginning with 'M'. |
| BRIDGET | (*Bored*) Moon. |
| PAUL | Man on the beach, shouting at us. |
| | (*The rhythm picks up again*) |
| BRIDGET | We strained to hear him. |

| | |
|---|---|
| VICKI | What did he call? |
| MARK | 'The Peace of God be with you all!' |
| PAUL | A piece of cod! He's out by a mile. |
| MARK | Then he said, 'Friends have you caught a pile?' |
| BRIDGET | (*Shouting back to shore*) We haven't enough for a sea-food stir-fry. |
| | Who do you think you are? |
| | (*All*) Captain Birdseye? |
| MARK | 'Throw your nets on the other side!' |
| VICKI | Give us a break – do you think we haven't tried? |
| PAUL | Now listen, pal, let's get one thing clear, |
| | I'm not quite sure what's going on here, |
| | We're members of the Fisherman's Federation |
| | And got there without your recommendation. |
| MARK | 'Throw your nets to the right!' |
| VICKI | He means to starboard. |
| BRIDGET | One more try, then back to harbour. |
| | Here you are, mate, this one's for you! |
| PAUL | We gathered the nets up, swung and threw. |
| | (*Silence. They wait, watching the water. Then with increasing urgency the rhythm returns*) |
| VICKI | Up from the deep came a flop and a splish |
| | In seconds, the sea was leaping with fish. |
| MARK | Turbot and bloater (*Vicki*) haddock and plaice, |
| BRIDGET | Spotted and flat (*Mark*) with an ugly face. |
| PAUL | Sea bass and flounder, red mullet and carp, |
| VICKI | Lobster and even (*Bridget*) a hammerhead shark! |
| MARK | As we struggled to pull the nets aboard |
| | Someone said softly: |
| PAUL | It is. It's the Lord! |
| BRIDGET | Peter looked up, crossed the deck in a flash |
| | And jumped overboard with an almighty splash. |
| MARK | All hands to the ropes! |

VICKI    We set to and followed,
         Heading for land – we sailed, he wallowed.
         (*The rhythm stops again as they mime bringing the
         boat up onto the beach. They all crouch around the
         'fire', facing the audience, blowing on their hands
         and unsure of how they should react to the presence
         of Jesus*)

PAUL     Up on the beach there was breakfast cooking.
         We stood round the fire, talking and looking.

BRIDGET  Jesus, who we'd seen dead in the ground
         Was grilling fish and handing bread round.

MARK     He said: 'Remember I made you fishers of men?
         You can't go back to catching crabs again.

VICKI    Forget your targets and EU quotas,
         Chuck out your stripey aprons and boaters.

PAUL     Sell your nets! You have my permission.
         And then do this – it's the great commission:

MARK     Tell my story in every nation
         Spread my message to all creation.
         (*The actors scramble back into the boat*)

BRIDGET  To every land that by sea is lapped
         This is the word, take it open or wrapped:

VICKI    God is doing something new!

PAUL     Watch out! Listen up! It could be YOU!'
         (*All repeat and fade last line*)

# Cosy-anity
## by Paul Birch with Paul Burbridge

FATHER *a man in his late thirties, hearty yet repressed*
JEREMY *his nine-year-old son, intelligent and enthusiastic*
MOTHER *a healthy, dependable woman in her early thirties*
ANNE *their two-year-old daughter, not as cute as her parents would like*

A Christmas sketch – but this one carries a health warning: it will not deepen anyone's understanding of the famous events in Bethlehem two thousand years ago, nor will it inspire worship, nor contribute to the special atmosphere of a candlelit carol service. It is deliberately intended as a satire on the whole commercial mish-mash of sentimental, quasi-religious ideas that Christmas has become in many people's minds. The entire Christmas season seems to have abandoned the truth about the poverty and hardship of Jesus' birth, replacing it with a cloying nostalgia trip for the ideal Christmas image, where Mary and Joseph are obviously just like all the rest in a well-scrubbed, beaming Middle England, full of glowing firesides, sturdy families and the smug cosy-ness of wealth.

And here is that very family. A very English family with all the sickening good health of the 1940s Ladybird books. The characterisations are exaggerated, the accents clipped and artificial.

With fixed expressions of domestic enthusiasm they speak, as it were, in a series of still pictures from the family photo album. Each change of pose is indicated in the script and accompanied by jolly snatches of that good old Christmas favourite 'A Partridge in a Pear Tree'.

# Cosy-anity

ALL      (*Singing in harmony*) Three French hens, two turtle doves, and a partridge in a pear tree!
(*The family group together for the first picture*)

FATHER      Well, family . . . here we all are at Christmas time, with a lovely log fire and mistletoe – all one big happy family. And, oh – look! There's my boy, Jeremy.

JEREMY      (*Shadow boxing*) Hello, father! Grin, grin. Lots of cheeky tomfoolery.

FATHER      (*Also shadow boxing*) Hello, Jeremy, you little scamp, you.

MOTHER      Oh, you two boys! Be nice now – it is Christmas, after all.

FATHER      Why, it's my lovely wife, Marion. And may I say you're looking such a lovely dumpling this fine day, my dear.

MOTHER      Thank you, dear. (*To Jeremy*) And how's my lovely little boy, Jeremy? (*She kisses him on the forehead*) And my pretty little gel, Anne. Tell everyone how old are you, Anne?

ANNE      (*Removing thumb from mouth momentarily*) Two!

MOTHER      And do you have some new words for Daddy, Anne?

ANNE      Smoking jacket.

MOTHER      That's right!

JEREMY      Oh, mother. You are the best.

MOTHER      No, dear. You're the best.

FATHER      No, family. We're the best!

JEREMY      (*Excessively cute*) Let's have a family hug.

153

(*They have a family hug, making lots of sickly noises*)

| | |
|---|---|
| JEREMY | Father? |
| FATHER | Yes, little man? |
| JEREMY | I just wanted to say . . . I love you. |
| FATHER | (*Slightly embarrassed*) Yes, that's the spirit, Jeremy. |
| MOTHER | I think I'm going to cry. |
| FATHER | Oh, no. You mustn't cry after such a finely cooked Christmas meal! |
| JEREMY | It was cool! |

(*Mother and father are deeply shocked*)

| | |
|---|---|
| FATHER | (*Suddenly vehement*) Jeremy! How could you use language like that in this house? We do not use Americanisms like that here! What do you say? |
| MOTHER | Answer your father. |
| JEREMY | Sorry, mother. Sorry, father. |
| MOTHER | That's better, Jeremy. We will have proper English spoken in this house, or none at all. |
| FATHER | Proper English! |

(*Jeremy begins to cry*)

| | |
|---|---|
| FATHER | Pull yourself together, Jeremy. |
| MOTHER | I think our baby needs a jolly good hug. |

(*They hug him, again making sickly noises*)

| | |
|---|---|
| JEREMY | I'm sorry for crying, Pop. |
| FATHER | That's all right, son. |

(*They move into another pose, singing:*)

| | |
|---|---|
| ALL | Ten lords a leaping, nine ladies dancing . . . |

(*Freeze*)

| | |
|---|---|
| FATHER | I think it's time, dear. |

(*He gives an outrageous wink to Marion*)

| | |
|---|---|
| MOTHER | I think so too, dear. |

(*She returns the outrageous wink*)

FATHER          Look behind the lounge suite, Jeremy. You might find a surprise.

JEREMY          (*Beside himself with excitement*) Oh boy oh boy oh boy! Is it a (*without pausing*) master blaster Nintendo Playstation with supergrip joystick and super street fighting Mario wars?

MOTHER          Well . . . take a look, dear.

JEREMY          (*Pulling out very two-dimensional props*) Oh, father, mother! What is it?

MOTHER          Don't you see? It's your very own set of colouring crayons.

FATHER          And a scrap book.

JEREMY          Just what I always wanted.

FATHER          Top hole, son.

MOTHER          And we haven't forgotten you, Anne.

ANNE            Smoking jacket?

MOTHER          Look. (*Handing her a similarly boring gift*) It's your first cookery book.

ANNE            Bottom!
                (*Mother gives a flat little embarrassed laugh. Nasty pause*)

JEREMY          Well, I'm exhausted. (*Exaggerated yawn*) I think I'll retire. It must be all of six o'clock.

MOTHER          But you know what comes first.

JEREMY          Is it the Jesus story, Pop?

FATHER          The Jesus story? Jesus who?

MOTHER          He's not that long-haired boy from down the street who fixes motor-cycles, is he?

FATHER          I should hope he isn't.

JEREMY          No, you know – the story you tell every year. The story of the nativity.
                (*Mother and father both feign astonishment*)

MOTHER          Oh, now I understand. You mean (*She says it as one rather strangely sounding name*) Bebbyjesus.

FATHER   You do say some silly things, Jeremy. It's Bebbyjesus. Not Jesus. Who ever heard of Jesus? (*He laughs*)

MOTHER   Jesus, indeed!
(*She laughs too*)
Come on then, dearest, do tell the Bebbyjesus story.
(*They move into a new photo-pose, singing:*)

ALL   Nine ladies dancing, eight maids a-milking, seven swans a-swimming . . .
(*Freeze*)

FATHER   Listen up, then, folks. There was once a lovely, lovely couple who were called Mary and Joseph, and they were on their way to be registered as good and honest voters. Unfortunately, because they had a house in the country, they had to go to the town, where all the people who actually worked for a living lived. So they travelled to . . . now, where did they travel to?

ANNE   Bottom?

MOTHER   No, dear.

JEREMY   Was it Bethlehem, Pater?

MOTHER   That's right, dear.

FATHER   Bethlehem. Correct. But what, can you tell me, did they travel in?

JEREMY   An ass!
(*Both parents gasp in shock*)

MOTHER   Jeremy!

FATHER   I can't believe you used that word in this house!

MOTHER   I'm ashamed of you. We do not use that word in this house. So common!

FATHER   What do you say, son?

| JEREMY | Sorry, father. Sorry, mother. But I don't under-stand. What *did* they travel in? |
|---|---|
| FATHER | Like all good decent folks, they drove to Bethlehem in a Volvo. A fine motor vehicle, the Volvo. And it was just as well, too, for Mary was expecting. |
| JEREMY | Expecting what? |
| MOTHER | Shush, Jeremy! |
| ANNE | Bottom! |
| MOTHER | Shush! |
| FATHER | The Bebbyjesus was due any day, and it was vital that Mary and Joseph find a lovely, hygienic place for them to stay. Now because their Volvo was a slow – but nevertheless reliable – machine, Mary and Joseph didn't reach Bethlehem until it was gone bedtime. All the Holiday Inns had been booked out. |
| JEREMY | And they had no place to stay! |
| MOTHER | Don't interrupt your father. |
| FATHER | That's right, pudding. They had no place to stay. (*They move into yet another pose, singing:*) |
| ALL | Eight maids a-milking, seven swans a-swimming, six geese a-laying . . . (*Freeze*) |
| FATHER | Except one. |
| JEREMY | And where was that? |
| FATHER | A little inn at the edge of the town. So Joseph knocked on the inn door and out came the innkeeper, saying (*in a highly cod common person's accent*), 'Merry Christmas, folks. What can I do you for?' Innkeepers are always rather vulgar people. And Joseph said, 'We are looking for a room for the night.' 'Sorry, sir,' chirped the |

innkeeper, 'all we have left is a stable, but it's clean and all the animals have been perfumed and vaccinated against all known diseases.'
(*New pose, singing:*)

ALL    Seven swans a-swimming, six geese a-laying, five gold rings!
(*Freeze*)

FATHER    And so Mary and Joseph spent the night in a very nice stable with thick carpets, hot showers, a nice comfy manger and cable TV. Now, there were three clever kings –

JEREMY    You mean shepherds, Daddy!

FATHER    No, Jeremy. I do not mean shepherds.

MOTHER    Don't contradict your father, Jeremy.

JEREMY    Sorry, Pop.

FATHER    Shepherds are for other people's nativities. We have kings in ours. Now, these three clever chaps were observing the stars, because they were clever and wanted to win the space race for Her Majesty the Queen, and while they were doing this they saw a great . . . big . . . shining . . .

ANNE    Smoking jacket!

FATHER    Yes, but what else did they see?

JEREMY    Umm . . . the Angel Gabriel!
(*More violent parental shock*)

FATHER    Jeremy! I will not have the occult mentioned in this house! No, son, who was it? Who did they see on the fateful night?

MOTHER    (*Prompting quietly*) Father Christmas.

JEREMY    Father Christmas!?

FATHER    Yes! Good old Santa Claus, off on his sleigh to give gifts to the children of the world.

JEREMY    Wow! Santa Claus!

| | |
|---|---|
| FATHER | Oh, yes. And who else brought Christmas gifts for Bebbyjesus? That's right, it was our old friends, those top-notch kings. |
| MOTHER | And do you remember what they brought? |
| JEREMY | Gold, frankincense and myrrh.<br>(*Mocking chuckles from the parents*) |
| MOTHER | The things you come up with, Jeremy! No, it was chocolate novelties, a train set and a sleeveless sweater. |
| JEREMY | But I thought they were paying tribute to the Son of God. |
| FATHER | Son of God? What nonsense! No, no, they gave him presents because Mary hadn't put up the Bebbyjesus' stocking. |
| JEREMY | Why not? |
| FATHER | I told you. The stable was centrally heated so there wasn't a fireplace. |
| JEREMY | Oh.<br>(*Final picture as they sing:*) |
| ALL | Four calling birds, three French hens, two turtle doves . . .<br>(*Freeze*) |
| FATHER | Anyway. The kings went back with Father Christmas to the Land of the Pixies and Mary and Joseph and Bebbyjesus got a proper home in the City. Where Bebbyjesus grew up to be a stock-broker, just like his dad. |
| MOTHER | That was a tip-top story, dearest. |
| FATHER | Just telling it like it was, dear. |
| ANNE | Bottom. |
| ALL | And a partridge in a pear tree!<br>(*Final family freeze with shiny grins*) |